Everyone wants to know – 'Does it really work?' and 'What sort of people join?'

In this book, *Dateline*, the world's leading computer dating agency, is happy to supply the answers – yes, it does work, and the people who join are people just like us.

ALL YOU NEED IS LOVE gives just a few of the thousands of happy endings which started with a *Dateline* questionnaire.

All You Need Is Love

DATELINE

edited by Ned Halley

SPHERE BOOKS LIMITED

SPHERE BOOKS LTD

Published by the Penguin Group
27 Wrights Lane, London W8 5TZ, England
Viking Penguin Inc., 40 West 23rd Street, New York, New York 10010, USA
Penguin Books Australia Ltd, Ringwood, Victoria, Australia
Penguin Books Canada Ltd, 2801 John Street, Markham, Ontario, Canada L3R
Penguin Books (NZ) Ltd, 182–190 Wairau Road, Auckland 10, New Zealand

Penguin Books Ltd, Registered Offices: Harmondsworth, Middlesex, England

Published by Sphere Books Ltd 1987
Reprinted 1989

Made and printed in Great Britain by
Richard Clay Ltd, Bungay, Suffolk
Filmset in Monophoto Photina

Contents

1

What people say about Dateline

Pauline Chandler, Press Officer of Dateline International, writes: Dateline computer dating is a subject which always generates interest. People are for it, against it, or just plain curious. But they are rarely indifferent to it.

We have all been in the situation of chatting in a group – during a meal, say – when the talk turns to what you do for a living. Sometimes my heart sinks when this happens, because I know I am likely to face a lively discussion about computer dating. And that tends to lead on to wider issues of single living, lone-liness and so on.

But it is a subject that fascinates everyone. After all, we have all been single at one time or another. And there is no question that it *is* sometimes difficult for single men and women to meet each other.

I particularly remember one occasion, when I was on holiday. Six of us around a table were talking about Dateline, and I was saying how difficult it can be for a man or a woman to meet someone with that certain 'sparkle'. I paused for breath and realized that everyone in the room, without exception, had fallen silent and was listening to what I was saying. You could have heard a pin drop!

When I got back to the office, three people from the holiday phoned me and asked for Dateline questionnaires.

Most people are genuinely interested in Dateline. But a few are very much against the idea of computer dating. Generally, they are people who have not tried it, or met anyone who has. Such critics tend to formulate ideas of the sort of people who, they imagine, join.

Their attitudes are apparent from such questions as: 'Why do people have to join Dateline?' 'Why can't they meet people in the "normal" way?' 'Surely they're "scraping the bottom of the barrel"?'

But the vast majority of people are curious to hear about Dateline – for they readily acknowledge that finding a life's partner is not that easy!

Everyone wants to know – 'Does it really work?' and 'What sort of people join?' It's good to be able to confirm that yes, it does work, and that the people who join are just like them. And that includes, now and then, members of Dateline's own staff . . . We're proud to say that we are directly responsible for marrying off two of our employees in the last three years. (Unfortunately they both moved away when they married, and left us. So matching Dateline staff can have its drawbacks.)

Dateline is the world's largest computer dating agency. As such, it's the first organization to which journalists turn when reporting topics such as dating, single people, loneliness and so on. Journalists can be pretty sceptical at first about computer dating, but once they have seen the Dateline system in operation they realize just how effective it can be.

I have had a journalist say to me, 'Have you *really*

got a computer?' (We showed it to her, installed in its own air-conditioned room.) But most reporters do accept that we couldn't possibly run an enterprise like Dateline without one. They are surprised, nevertheless, when they learn that some 3,000 people join Dateline every month; that we have the largest post-bag in the London borough of Kensington; that we spend a million pounds a year on advertising. But seeing is believing, which is why we are always happy to show people round our offices.

One major change that has taken place during Dateline's first twenty-one years is that people have become more and more willing to talk about how the system has helped them to find someone to settle down with. In the past, few of the huge numbers of people using Dateline would have dreamed of revealing their membership to anyone else.

Our advertising is always built around couples who have met through Dateline, and these couples are constantly being replaced by yet more with their own stories to tell. We are now in the remarkable position of having too many people who are willing to appear in our advertising. We are literally spoiled for choice. These people don't offer their stories to us for gain. They do so because they want others to know how Dateline worked for them – and therefore how it can work for people in similar situations. The conspiracy of silence has been broken. And the more they talk about it, the more they answer those two crucial questions – *yes, Dateline does work, and the sort of people who use it are just like you and me.*

'Help yourself'

If there's one piece of advice most Dateline members would like to pass on to anyone contemplating joining, it seems it would be to 'help yourself'.

'Dateline doesn't set the rules – you do. You can join for whatever you want to get out of it. If you want a relationship, it's there. If you want a friendship, it's there. But it's up to you to get your finger out and do it, because no one else is going to do it for you. I got out of it what I wanted, and if this relationship doesn't work out I'll do it again.'

– JOHN HOMER, BRIGHTON

'With Dateline, if at first you don't succeed, then try, try again. If someone turns you down, try someone else and keep going. Just keep going, because it *does* work.'

– ELAINE PRITCHARD, SOMERSET

'Don't allow yourself to be put off by what anybody says. If you feel you want to join Dateline, just go ahead. There's such a lot to be gained in life. It's turned my life completely upside down!'

– KERRY STONE, BATH

'To anybody joining Dateline I'd say don't be disappointed if you don't find somebody straight away. It's just a matter of persevering with letters really, and not expecting everybody to reply.'

– PAM CLARK, LEEDS

Another area of frequent comment about Dateline is the happy one of how enjoyable membership can be. Not every-

4

one joins in quest of a permanent relationship, and some are there simply for a broader social life.

'I went out with an awful lot of people. The majority of them were really nice, and Dateline certainly broadened my social scene. I had a great time. My family couldn't believe it – I was never home.'

– BARBARA REYNOLDS, ESSEX

'As a way for young people to meet and have a good time, then I would definitely say yes, join Dateline. I met genuine men who honestly and truly wanted to meet new people as much as I did, who wanted to make *friends* and have a good time.'

– SUE CHURCH, IPSWICH

'When I told my friends that all these men were phoning up and asking me out they said "If you've got any spares, you can pass them on!" They were all quite surprised at what a good time you do have with Dateline.'

– JEANNE ALEXANDER, WORTHING

'It was fun meeting new people. It definitely helped me as a person. Just meeting other folk and discussing their problems and so on made me feel – well, I wasn't so alone.'

– RON WATT, SCOTLAND

For other Dateline members, who perhaps joined purely for friendship, there have often been very pleasant surprises in store.

'Joining Dateline was the only way I could get out and about and find someone. I hoped that I might meet some people for friends. The fact that I might marry

5

someone was out of this world – just absurd – but it was just something that happened.'

– KATIE BROOKBANK, SUTTON

'If I had flown to the moon, I don't think it could have changed my life as much as Dateline has. I joined to enjoy myself, which I did, but then ten weeks after I joined I met Martin and fell head over heels in love.'

– SUE RIDDLE, IPSWICH

'I joined Dateline because I thought I'd probably meet lots of people. I didn't really think about marrying anyone!'

– JULIE STONE, BATH

While membership can have its surprises, however, there is still a common thread of realism among those who join Dateline. Many members have commented on the practical virtues of the computer-matching principle, and on the benefits of joining in a large network.

'Dateline worked for me. I think there are quite a few cowboy outfits around and people are worried for that reason. But as far as I am concerned it worked perfectly well. There were enough people in it and enough range and variety to be able to pick out the right person.'

– PHILIP WENTWORTH, GLOUCESTERSHIRE

'I'm never shy about admitting that I met my husband by computer. It may sound unromantic, but it's logical and it *works*. I'm sure it's the best thing anybody can do. Not everyone is going to meet their life partner, but it's such a logical way of meeting people you've got things in common with. You know they're in the market too for a relationship – if only a friendship – instead of picking someone up in a pub, about whom you know nothing.'

– CINDY SMITH, LONDON

'Meeting people through Dateline is not very different from meeting someone in a disco, except that the person is more likely to be on your wavelength. Dateline gives you a chance of making something out of the meeting instead of it being just another one-night stand, which I didn't want any more.'

– PETER HAMNETT, LANCASHIRE

'As I see it, I wouldn't have chosen Andrew if I'd seen him over the other side of a disco. But meeting through Dateline you get to know their personality and you get on pretty well with the ones you're matched up with. We got on so well I couldn't believe it.'

– JACKIE WEBB, CORNWALL

Finally, to that question 'What sort of people join Dateline?' It's a question not only asked by those who are mildly curious about the system, but by those who join Dateline, too. These are a few of the comments made by members who have found the answer.

'Everybody I corresponded with or met was perfectly normal, perfectly ordinary – not the weirdos or ogres that you might think would go in for something like computer dating. It opens your eyes up really, because there's no excuse for anybody to be lonely. There are millions of people who are only too happy to meet you or ring you up. You may have visions of them being "leftovers", but nothing could be further from the truth.'

— GRAHAM ALEXANDER, WORTHING

'The thing about Dateline is that everyone who writes to you is in the same position. It's a very easy way of meeting someone in your age group who likes what you like.'

— RON CROW, LONDON

'Some people think if you join Dateline you'll meet freaks, but that's not true. You'll meet people who are quite normal — just like yourself.'

— MARK SLATER, SCOTLAND

'I think if I expected anything I probably thought the people who joined Dateline wouldn't be particularly attractive, or there would be something wrong with them. I was agreeably surprised that Barbara was quite an attractive person. When I started talking to her I found she was a *very* attractive person.'

— MICHAEL BROWN, ROMFORD

'I thought she was too attractive to be a member of Dateline!'

— TIM SMITH, NORFOLK

'The old-fashioned idea of a dating agency being only for those who are "hard up" for companionship and who have to "resort" to this form of meeting other people is totally wrong. I don't feel embarrassed about being a member of Dateline. It's fun!'

— NORMA WILLIAMS, LONDON

2
Single no more

Single people have got it made. These days, they have plenty of opportunity to meet each other. There are plenty of prospective partners to choose from. And there are obvious places to find them: the pub, the disco, the wine bar. And so on.

That's the way almost everyone who *isn't* single sees it, anyway. Until, that is, they take the trouble to talk to the single people they know. Then they discover that nothing has really changed. It's still just as difficult for single people to meet suitable partners now as it has ever been. Maybe even more so.

Young men have a particularly hard time of it. In Britain, there are twice as many single men under twenty-five as there are single women. Very nice for the girls. But where do the boys go to find eligible young women?

The pendulum, it must be said, swings the other way as men enter their thirties, forties and fifties. But that's cold comfort to a young man of twenty-three in search of a woman with whom to settle down.

Today's itinerant lifestyle presents a problem for single people seeking a partner. Take graduates, for example. Very often they leave their home town and their friends – probably for the first time – and they spend the next three or four years in education making a whole new set of acquaintances. But when they leave college they are unlikely to find a job in either their university town or their home town. They must start all over, yet again, in a strange place where they know no one.

Many single people meet their partner at work. Others, in the many 'single-sex' occupations, are not so lucky.

Engineers, teachers, nurses, shopworkers – all can find it very hard to meet eligible people through their jobs. If their social lives don't bring them into contact with members of the opposite sex either, they've got a real problem. The lives of single men under forty tend to revolve round their work. And for very many of them, their evenings tend to revolve round the pub, where they congregate with nary a female in sight.

But single women have their troubles too. There is a growing sector of young, unmarried women in the UK who have responsible jobs, homes of their own – and find it hard to meet men who can match their achievements. It can be difficult even to find young men who can accept the successful lifestyles of such young women.

These women don't tend to go to the disco – even if they were to believe they would meet the right kind of man there (which they probably wouldn't). The same goes for the pub. So where do they go?

Commonly, they go out with girlfriends for meals, to the cinema, to the theatre. Or they go to health clubs, where they meet other women in the same circumstances – and very few eligible men.

Certainly a great many single people do still meet each other in the ways they always have done. But today's lifestyles, the evolving roles of men and women, mean that sometimes these traditional opportunities to meet simply do not arise. Single people may well have to make a special effort if they wish to find someone to settle down with – especially in the light of today's higher expectations.

Many single people accept that Mr or Mrs Right is unlikely to turn up purely as a matter of chance. Hence the increasing interest in dating agencies, introduction bureaux, 'contact' magazines and personal columns in newspapers and magazines.

And why not? Why should single people put less effort into finding a partner than they would into, say, buying a house or a car? The more people they meet, the more likely they are to find the man or woman who is right for them.

And *anything* which gets single people out and meeting each other has surely got to be a very good thing.

PAULINE CHANDLER,
PRESS OFFICER, DATELINE INTERNATIONAL

Olga and Richard

At forty, Olga Alexander knew she stood at a crossroads in her life. At the age when life is supposed to begin, she was quite happily single – albeit with a few broken relationships behind her. But she nevertheless did ponder the possibility of marriage. Was it what she wanted, or would she prefer to stay single?

She joined Dateline, she says, to find out.

'At the time,' said Olga, a cello teacher from Winchester in Hampshire, 'I thought either it's going to confirm that I'm OK as I am, or that I'm not OK as I am!'

The week before Olga joined, Richard Knight, aged forty-five, had done so too. A bank manager from Havant, also in Hampshire, Richard had been separated from his wife for a year.

'It had been rather a traumatic time for me,' Richard recalled. 'I was leaning very heavily on the few personal friends I had, and meeting very few other people. I really couldn't see how I could increase my circle of friends. That's really the reason I joined Dateline.'

Richard met four women before Dateline gave his name to Olga.

'None of them really fired me with great enthusiasm,' he smiled.

Olga wrote to Richard, and he telephoned her. He had to do so several times before finding her at home – finally reaching her on a Sunday afternoon.

Since they were both free that day, they got together to take Olga's dogs for a walk.

'Olga and I seemed to have a certain rapport.'

'We enjoyed ourselves,' said Olga. 'I liked him. I did feel I was talking to a stranger, but the only way I can discover a person is to do something active and talk. I'm not a person to sit over drinks and chatter.'

So Richard's suggestion of a walk with the dogs could not have been a better one.

'Olga and I seemed to have a certain rapport,' he said. 'Things seemed to click. The first meeting went very well – well enough for me to invite Olga to Verdi's *Requiem* at the Portsmouth Guildhall the following Saturday. She accepted – and I think the

12

intervening week has been the longest time that we have been apart ever since!'

For Richard, the *Requiem* was a very special night. Quite apart from the beautiful music, it was on that occasion that he realized he liked Olga very much indeed.

'Afterwards we went to a wine bar to have a snack and a drink, to talk and perhaps to get to know each other a little more,' Richard remembered. 'Everything seemed to go very naturally. Very well indeed. Then I invited her back to my house for a coffee and to listen to a couple of records before she went home to Winchester.'

A week later Olga invited him to dinner at her home.

'I feel that we ought to have a future together.'

'I liked his personality,' she said. 'It's difficult to say why you hit it off with one person and not another. Probably his sense of humour. And he gets on so well with my dogs. There are no airs and graces about him ... I just like him.'

They began to see each other three or four times a week. It was on their twelfth meeting – they were both counting – when Olga and Richard were together in her drawing room ('She was sitting on my knee at the time!' Richard laughed) that he asked her to marry him.

'We were talking about how well we seemed to get on,' he said, 'and how we had both had deep, traumatic experiences of our own in each of our lives, and this possibly helped us understand each other.

13

'Suddenly I said, "I wonder how this is going to affect our future?"'

'How do you mean?' Olga had asked him.

'I feel that we ought to have a future together,' Richard had promptly replied.

'From there,' he said, 'it was only a short step for me to ask her to marry me. And she immediately accepted.'

'I wasn't expecting his proposal when it came, but I was expecting it would be a long-term relationship,' said Olga.

She paused. 'No . . . I knew. I suppose we have a sixth sense. Richard meant a lot. Meant something different from other people. And I'm not a person to knock around with people just for the sake of it.'

Both of them were slightly dazed by the speed of their attachment.

'I tend to be a person who follows powerful hunches.'

'Life is very strange and you do some unexpected things,' mused Olga. 'Of the people I met, Richard was the one in the worst situation. He still had a wife, he had two children at private school. I had met a single chap who was ideal and another chap who was free. But of the three I wouldn't have chosen the other two. Not for anything.

'I think we have a sixth sense in life. I think if you follow a very strong hunch – and I tend to be a person who follows powerful hunches and invariably find I am right – well . . . Richard was a very strong hunch.'

She laughed. 'A big one, too. He's six-foot-four!'

Said Richard: 'If anybody had told me three months previously that I would be engaged in the next few weeks, I would have told them they were absolutely crazy. I had no intention of getting married again at that time. Absolutely none. I had had a very happy marriage for eighteen years and I have two super children. I would have felt I couldn't possibly improve on that marriage.

'I suppose right from the word go, Olga and I were very frank. We talked very openly with each other and we just held nothing back about our lives. We really do have a lot in common in our attitudes to life. Olga has had an unhappy time and it's left a scar, the same way as the break-up of my marriage has left a scar. We have both been able to help each other in this respect.'

Olga and Richard were planning to marry as soon as he is free to do so. In the mean time, arrangements are in hand for their future together. Single, as far as they are both concerned, is something they no longer care to be.

Barry and Deborah

Barry and Deborah Gregory are a warm, happy young couple. They have lately bought their first home, which they share with their new baby, John James. Not long ago, however, they were both reluctant singles — wondering just how they were ever going to be anything else.

'I was very lonely,' said Deborah, an attractive brunette, now twenty-one. 'I hardly ever went out. I just watched television at home most of the time.'

She worked in an old people's home, a job which she loved, but which contributed little to her social life. 'I'd moved to a new area to work there, and left my friends behind, too,' she said. 'And where I lived was very rural, very quiet.'

It was a girlfriend of Deborah's brother who encouraged her to join Dateline – which, after some reluctance, she did.

'I just watched TV at home most of the time.'

'I was twenty-three when I joined Dateline,' said Barry, a slim, soft-spoken Hampshire man. 'I was very isolated in my small village. Although I worked as a salesman for an electrical company, I didn't meet many girls.'

Deborah went out with three of her contacts before she heard from Barry. Although he lived quite a distance away, she liked the way he expressed himself in the letter he wrote her. She replied promptly. Barry telephoned her – and they talked for no less than two hours.

'We hit it off straight away,' said Barry. 'Somehow we just knew what to talk to each other about.'

Easter was imminent, and they agreed that Barry would travel to Deborah's home on Good Friday to meet her and her family.

'We met at the station and we were both half an hour early,' Deborah remembered. 'Barry told me he would be wearing a bright red shirt, so I would be able to recognize him. But it seemed to me that just about

16

every man was wearing a bright red shirt that day!'

Although they had never met, Deborah was right first time when she thought she had spotted him.

'I just *knew* it was him,' she smiled.

He greeted her with a bunch of rather wilted tulips. The flowers were actually for Deborah's mother.

'I liked that,' Deborah said. 'None of the others had thought about my mum.'

By the end of the day, the couple felt as if they had known each other for years. Barry had to work the following day, but he eagerly offered to travel back the next evening. They agreed that he should spend the rest of the weekend with her and her family.

'None of the others had thought about my mum'

After Easter their romance blossomed. They phoned each other daily ('the bills were enormous' laughed Deborah) and met every weekend. Within just a couple of weeks they were discussing an engagement.

'Actually, Deborah proposed to me,' said Barry, grinning at his wife.

'It's true,' she replied. 'I got a few drinks down him and then quietly asked him, "Why don't we get engaged?" And he said "Yes, why not?"'

Their wedding is now an already mellowing memory, but Deborah's silk bouquet still decorates the mantelpiece of their neat terraced house.

Deborah takes a deep and simple pleasure in her new life.

'It's changed so quickly. One minute I was depressed,

just watching television when I wasn't working. Now I've got a husband and a baby. My life is so busy – and I am very happy.'

'I got a few drinks down him then quietly asked him . . .'

'My life used to be very basic,' said Barry. 'Nine-to-five job, and home to village social life. I was beginning to worry that I would never find anyone, and I didn't want to be single all my life. Deborah and I love being together, and we know our marriage is absolutely right.'

Alan and Glenda

By postponing their first date on three successive occasions, Glenda Campbell made an important discovery about Alan Colbeck.

'Because of commitments at work, I really did have to put him off,' remembered Glenda, a thirty-nine-year-old legal secretary from Leeds. 'And what I discovered about him in the process was that he was a very patient and tolerant person! He just said each time: "OK, I'll arrange to meet you some other time." I liked him from the telephone conversations we had, and I wrote to him and apologized for having put him off for what sounded like feeble excuses.'

For his part, Alan – a thirty-six-year-old machine operator – gave her the benefit of the doubt. He had already met a number of women through Dateline, and was hoping – increasingly despairingly by now – to find a partner for life.

'Naturally I did wonder if all what she was telling me was true or not,' he said. 'But I did like her voice over the phone – and that's what kept me going. As a matter of fact, I felt that Glenda might be my last shot.'

What Alan didn't know about Glenda was that she had emphatically *not* joined Dateine in a quest for a life partner. She merely wanted to meet people to share her social life with – to get her out of the rut of pub and club nights she had slipped into. She had no interest in marriage whatsoever.

'I felt that Glenda might be my last shot.'

Fortunately for both of them, she didn't reveal her feelings on this score when, eventually, she and Alan had their first meeting. At their rendezvous, the station at Alan's home town of Wakefield, Glenda recognized him from the photograph he had sent her.

'I knew he had a beard and spectacles,' she recalled. 'Beards bring me out in a rash, but I liked him anyway!'

Their encounter was a success – in an understated way.

'He was quiet,' Glenda said, 'but he was very pleasant, and easy to talk to. I didn't know whether he would ask me out again, so I told him I would like to see him again if he would like to see me. He said he would.'

That second date, a week later, was very nearly postponed like the first. Glenda caught a virus which made her feel pretty low, and when Alan phoned to confirm their arrangement for the day she admitted to him that she was unwell ... did he want to cancel?

'No,' he told her firmly. 'I'll come over anyway.'

Alan took her out for a drive, visiting some of his favourite spots for fishing – his preferred leisure pursuit. Despite still feeling a little low, Glenda had a marvellous time.

'We got on so well,' she remembers, 'that I really didn't want him to leave that night.'

'It would have broken my heart if he hadn't wanted to see me again.'

Alan, too, was realizing that Glenda was growing on him more and more.

'I felt so relaxed with her – much more so than with any of the others I had met,' he said. 'I felt able to be myself all the time.'

Their next outing – to a stately home – was another success.

'By then I knew I wanted to know him a lot more. I think it would have broken my heart if he hadn't wanted to see me again,' Glenda recalled with a smile.

She had no cause to fear, however, for by this stage Alan felt just the same.

By now the time for Alan to go off on a fishing holiday to Scotland – arranged long beforehand with a friend – was drawing near.

'I didn't particularly want to go,' Alan remembered, 'but I was committed.'

Shortly before departing, he decided he must tell Glenda of his desire for marriage. He broached the subject somewhat tentatively: 'Well, I don't think we'll mess about any more,' he told her. 'I think it would be nice if you had a ring on your finger.'

She put her misgivings about marriage promptly aside – and agreed with him.

'It's like looking for a needle in a haystack – but I *found* one!'

'Although I'd been against marriage for a long, long time, I had no hestitation at the idea of tying the knot and tripping down the aisle with Alan,' said Glenda. 'I *want* to be married to him, to *be* with him.'

They became formally engaged as soon as Alan returned from Scotland ('It was five days – and it seemed like months,' Alan recalled with a laugh). Altogether it had only been a month since they had first met.

Alan and Glenda are planning their wedding for the near future, both of them thrilled at the happiness they have found – but could so easily have missed had it not been for Alan's patience.

Alan freely admits that he was close to giving up his search for a partner through Dateline, but now he counsels perseverance.

'Keep going. Keep at it,' he said. 'It's like looking for a needle in a haystack – but I managed to find one!'

Cindy and Tony

Cindy Palmer and Tony Smith met each other through Dateline in its early days. Back in 1970, the agency was only four years old, and Cindy and Tony recently celebrated thirteen years of marriage by writing to Dateline with their story.

When Cindy joined Dateline she was twenty-eight, living in West Hampstead, London, and working as a director's secretary in a large photographic company.

She was surrounded daily by older, attractive men (just her type, she admitted), but they were invariably married.

'I got bored with getting involved with men I shouldn't,' said Cindy. 'I wasn't interested in men of my own age; they seemed immature.'

Cindy was finding it increasingly difficult to make a happy social life for herself. Most of her female friends were married, or had steady relationships. So she joined Dateline – in the hope that at least she would meet some men with interests akin to her own.

'I went out with quite a few people – about a dozen – but although they matched up very well in terms of common interests, there were none I felt really drawn to.'

Nevertheless, her social life had become dramatically more active. 'At one time, I was going out with six different people! It was quite a hectic time.'

Three months after she joined, Cindy was contacted by Tony Smith. An electronics engineer from Streatham in south London, thirty-three-year-old Tony had recently ended a very close relationship, and felt he needed to get back into the ways of taking women out.

'I'm a bit shy,' he confessed. 'Having no sisters, I found women pretty mysterious. I had great difficulty in picking up young ladies!'

'We went out for dinner on our first date to a nice little restaurant,' Cindy recalled. 'Tony was very quiet and shy, but I thought he had a nice, kind, sensitive face – and I was glad we had so much in common. But he wasn't very forthcoming. I didn't really feel we got to know each other on our first date.'

'He was obviously intelligent.'

Difficult as Tony was to get to know, Cindy set great store by the fact that they had so much in common. They were both, for example, particularly fond of classical music.

'I remember it particularly,' said Cindy, 'because it's so rare to find someone who enjoys serious classical music as much as serious popular music. That meant a lot to me. He was obviously intelligent, and we could talk about all sorts of things. But I could never get close to him.'

Before long, Cindy was to discover why.

Despite having tried to disentangle himself from his former relationship, Tony was still very much involved with his girlfriend of old.

'It wasn't really finished,' he admitted. 'I know this affected my behaviour with Cindy. I didn't try to get close to her.'

Five months after they started seeing each other, the blow fell.

Tony confessed to Cindy that he was still seeing

the other girl – and that they were going to be married.

'He had seemed pretty keen on me, I thought,' said Cindy. 'Then one day he tells me out of the blue that another girl he was seeing had agreed to become engaged to him! This quiet boy had been two-timing me – and it was quite a blow to my ego.

'He had seemed pretty keen on me, I thought.'

'I was not used to being the one who was told it was over,' she added wryly. 'To be honest, it was usually the other way round.'

Cindy missed Tony. Not only had his rejection bruised her self-esteem, but she had very much enjoyed going out with him and sharing their mutual interests. But she tried to put the episode behind her, and continued seeing two or three different men through Dateline.

'Certainly I had a very lively and enjoyable social life. But I did still yearn to find someone with whom I could share a permanent relationship.'

Tony's resurrected engagement didn't work out at all, and within a few weeks he ended the relationship once and for all. He continued his Dateline membership too, and soon rebuilt a busy social life.

'I was going out with three or four girls. But all the time Cindy's image was in the background. She was the one I remembered. Not only because of her appearance, but because we had so much in common. I'd always said to her she was too good to be true!'

24

An unlikely event now intervened. Tony was prosecuted for driving 'over the limit' in the autumn of 1971, and consequently lost his licence. This naturally curtailed his mobility, and it meant too that anyone he went out with would have to be fairly close to home.

'I was still feeling a bit "stung"'

That, at least, was the way Tony saw it. It gave him the excuse he needed; he wrote to Cindy, explaining that things had not worked out with his fiancée, that everything was now over between them. And he wanted to see Cindy again.

'I was still feeling a bit "stung" after his unexpected ending of our relationship,' said Cindy. 'I thought he had a cheek to drop me and then months later write to me expecting me to see him again. So I didn't reply to his letter for several days.

'But something told me that I was at an important crossroads in my life. That it was vitally important for me to take the right direction this time. Tony and I had so many interests in common, yet I felt I hardly knew him. Surely it was worth giving our relationship another try. and perhaps it would turn into something deeper.'

Cindy wrote Tony a guarded letter. She said she did not want to become involved with him again if he was still carrying a torch for the girl who had turned him down. He replied immediately that it wasn't like that at all. Things just hadn't worked out between them – and he could not get Cindy out of his mind.

So it was that in September 1971. Cindy and Tony

took up again where they had left off. And from their first encounter, everything was very different between them.

'It was obviously because Tony had broken up with the other girl,' said Cindy. 'He was a bit upset, but not broken-hearted, and was clearly keen to start another relationship. It was apparent that he was pleased I was still available and, building on our friendship, we fairly quickly became lovers.'

Without the other girl on his mind, Tony was much more open and forthcoming in his conversation and his feelings.

'He was so much more outgoing,' said Cindy. 'He wasn't nearly so shy, and he had more depths than I had realized. There was a lot more to him than I had first assumed.'

'He had more depths to him than I had realized.'

By her own admission, Cindy was not keen on the idea of marriage. But Tony changed all that.

They both recall the proposal – even if they disagree on the details.

Cindy says they were having a row at the time, but Tony doesn't remember that. It seems the couple had frequent 'animated discussions' on the fact that Tony could not be sure of Cindy's feelings towards him.

Tired of these exchanges, and – as they both recall – to the background of Beethoven's *Pastoral* symphony on the hi-fi, Cindy finally said: 'This is ridiculous. You don't seem to believe I feel the same about you – so I think we ought to get married!'

Cindy laughed at the memory.

'I couldn't believe I'd actually said it. I'd never been too keen on getting married. But the way the relationship was going, I thought it was the best way of proving I was serious about him.'

Tony was quick to recover from his amazement – and equally quick about the arrangements. He and Cindy were married the following week at Hampstead Register Office. It was April 1972, six months after their reunion.

Cindy and Tony moved out to Maidstone in Kent, and in 1980 their son James was born. Their marriage has brought them both a great deal of happiness and contentment.

'I firmly believe that the main reason our marriage has been so happy and has survived all the various troubles which have beset us in the past years is because we began as friends with shared views and interests. Not until after that did we become lovers,' said Cindy. 'So many people fall in love the other way round. Then, when the physical passion wanes they realize that they have nothing else in common – and their relationship is dead.'

3

With a little help . . .

A strand that runs through the stories of very many Dateline members is that of the natural nervousness they confess to, not just in encountering strangers, but in actually joining up in the first place.

Dateline members are consequently very often talked into 'taking the plunge' (a very common phrase in these annals!) by a third party. It may be a parent – daughters are frequently encouraged by mothers – or a friend. Colleagues at work, too, tend to be keen to encourage single workmates. And are then agog, of course, to hear all about the progress made . . .

The following stories – just a handful of the hundreds that began in the same way – illustrate well how dramatically the life of reluctant romantics can be changed. With a little help from their friends.

Dennis and Nancy

Londoner Nancy Sutton felt she was quite content, aged forty-seven, to be on her own. She had been divorced three years earlier, and had a job as a warden in sheltered accommodation for the elderly.

One of her tenants, however, was not convinced that the solitary life was for Nancy. That tenant was Mrs

Lamb, who not only nagged Nancy unmercifully about never going out, but went further . . .

'She gave me an application form for Dateline out of the *TV Times*,' said Nancy. 'I took it from her, put it down somewhere and then lost it. So she gave me another one!'

In the end, Nancy had to give in – and joined.

Armed with a list of six names, she nevertheless continued to prevaricate, and did nothing to make contact for nearly four months. But Mrs Lamb wanted to know how Nancy was getting on. Nancy showed her the list.

'Dennis somehow kept coming into my mind.'

'Here, *you* sort them out,' she said. 'You pick out three and I'll write little notes to them.'

The three notes, co-written with Mrs Lamb, produced two replies. One was from Dennis Cox.

A fifty-five-year-old engineer, Dennis had already met several women through Dateline. 'All very pleasant people,' he said – but none who had so far 'clicked'.

When he received Nancy's note, he rang her. They agreed he would pick her up the following week for a drink.

But Nancy chickened out.

'I phoned him up and made up a tale about relatives visiting,' she said sheepishly. 'During the week, however, Dennis somehow kept coming into my mind. I felt guilty – especially as I was going on holiday to Majorca, and knew I really should meet him before I went away.'

29

Guilt overcame nerves, and Nancy rang to arrange a date, just prior to her trip.

Dennis was impressed with her.

'I found it easy to talk to her,' he remembered. 'I thought she was an interesting and nice person.'

Nancy was similarly taken with Dennis, and quickly accepted when he suggested another meeting for the next evening – the eve of her departure for Majorca.

'The meal we had that night was a disaster,' said Nancy, laughing.

'The meal we had that night was a disaster.'

What Dennis did not know was that Nancy was a virtual vegetarian – and he took her to a carvery.

'I left most of the food,' Nancy recalled. 'But I enjoyed the company.'

On holiday, Nancy's mind was in a turmoil.

'I was half deciding to go back to my ex-husband,' she confessed.

But she found that her thoughts turned more and more to Dennis.

'The first one I phoned from the airport when I got back was Dennis. We met that evening, and from then on we saw each other almost daily – or at least when he could, as he had other lady friends at the time.'

'It was slowly dawning on me – though not that slowly – that Nancy was special,' Dennis remembered of this time.

A few weeks after her holiday, Dennis took Nancy to visit her mother in Winchester. He later took her to see relatives along the south coast. It was returning from one of these trips that Dennis quietly suggested to Nancy that they should live together.

Nancy hesitated, but he urged her not to answer straight away. She should think about it and let him know. That evening, he raised the subject again.

'He asked me to marry him,' said Nancy.

'I didn't mean just *living* together,' Dennis told her. 'I meant you to marry me.'

'I've even told my ex-husband to join.'

Still Nancy hesitated. She did agree, but said she felt it might be too soon. Dennis acknowledged her feelings, and they postponed their engagement for three months.

Nancy and Dennis were married in the local Methodist church a year after they first met. Nancy happily admits that joining Dateline turned out to be a wise move. She adds: 'But I'd tell people not to expect too much at first. Persevere, in other words. In fact, I've even told my ex-husband to join.'

Guest of honour at Nancy and Dennis's wedding was, of course, a delighted Mrs Lamb.

'After all,' says Nancy, 'it was really all down to her.'

Deborah and Frank

When she was twenty-two, Deborah Darwood came home to live with her mother in Catchgate, County Durham. She brought with her Mark, her two-year-old son; her second son, Christopher, was born four months later. She left behind her a ruined marriage to a British soldier stationed abroad.

Two years on, with the baby toddling and the unhappy memories receding, Deborah was beginning to sense the need for a new start.

'I don't like being on my own – I'm not cut out for it,' she admitted. 'I have to be needed by somebody, and I need somebody too.'

Deborah's mother, anxious for her happiness and well aware her daughter was too young to be staying at home day and night, encouraged her to join Dateline. And as the fee was beyond Deborah's means as a single parent, her mother paid it for her.

Deborah wrote to all the young men who were introduced, and was scrupulously honest about her domestic situation.

'I felt it was important they should know I was a single parent with two boys. And I must admit, this did seem to put some of them off.'

But by no means all. Deborah dated several contacts during the three months before she was sent the name of Frank Darwood.

Frank was twenty-five, an electrical engineer from Newcastle-upon-Tyne. The reply he sent to Deborah's initial letter impressed her.

'It was chatty. None of the others had been. They were more formal.'

But Deborah was determined to tread warily.

'I didn't want to meet him straight away and then be disappointed if we didn't have anything to talk about.'

Deborah and Frank exchanged fourteen letters before meeting. Writing the last of them, in which she mentioned that her birthday was coming up, Deborah finally decided that this would be the perfect occasion for them to meet.

'I thought to myself, here I am writing to a nice bloke, and yet I'm frightened to meet him. It was daft! So I wrote that I would hate to have to stay in on my birthday, and could we meet on the night of it? He wrote straight back and said yes!'

They arranged to meet at the Smith's Arms at Catchgate, very close to Deborah's home. Frank made an inspired start by sending her flowers and a birthday card by Interflora at midday.

'I thought about the idea of an instant family.'

Their evening meeting got off to an auspicious start, too. They had exchanged photographs – 'not very good ones' according to Deborah – so when she arrived at their rendezvous she recognized Frank at once.

'Our eyes met and that was it!' Deborah recalled. The first thing she remembers actually thinking about him was 'Oh. He smells nice.'

They spent the evening – until well after midnight – in animated conversation. It was the same two days later when they met once more.

'Again, we got on like a house on fire,' Frank remembered.

Two weeks now passed before they saw each other again, as Frank had a prearranged holiday.

'Every one of those days I was thinking about him,' said Deborah. 'I was worrying in case he might meet somebody else. Then, the day before he was due back, I got a postcard from him. It said "Miss you". It made my day!'

The couple took up where they had left off. Frank started to get to know Mark and Christopher. Deborah was amazed at how the boys took to him, even on their first meeting: 'Mark straight away went and sat right up against Frank – he just sat there and looked up at him. Christopher went up to him immediately too and started talking to him. I was surprised, because the baby wasn't used to men, with it being an all-female household.'

'The postcard said "Miss you". It made my day.'

'I thought about the whole idea of an instant family from the first time I met Deborah,' said Frank. 'I decided that I did not dislike the prospect – and I decided too that I was really in love with Deborah.'

It was young Mark who first voiced the subject of marriage. With all the innocent directness of a four-year-old, he asked Frank: 'Are you going to come and be my Daddy?'

Frank tried to explain the situation as best he could. Mark's artless question had meanwhile struck a chord with Deborah.

'I suddenly realized just how much I wished it would happen,' she recalled. 'I also realized that if I waited for Frank to ask I might wait for ever!'

It was now six weeks since the couple had first met, and Deborah resolved to propose. She did so when they were washing Frank's car together.

'I had been saying all day that I had a question to ask him that evening. I think he'd guessed, but anyway I said, "Are you to going to marry me then?"

'He said, "I don't know. I'll have to think about it."'

Deborah remembers her surprise – and despair – at his words: 'I thought, "That's it. He's not interested. He doesn't think it's a good idea."'

But Deborah need not have worried. The following day Frank came to the point.

'So will you marry me?' he asked.

'You don't have to live on your own.'

'I think he just wanted to be the one who did the asking,' said Deborah.

Frank agreed: 'I felt better if I did myself.'

As for Deborah, she's convinced that her mother's gift of a Dateline membership was just about the best present she's ever had. It meant to her what she feels it would mean to countless others: 'You don't have to live on your own; you'll find there's always somebody who wants to be loved.'

Fiona and Ron

Ron Watt admits that he took his time – 'years, in actual fact' – over joining Dateline. A house sales officer from Midcalder, West Lothian in Scotland, most of Ron's friends were married by the time he was twenty-nine – and it was two of them who finally persuaded Ron of the wisdom of computer dating.

'It's very hard to meet people when you don't really want to go to a disco or for a drink on your own,' said Ron, 'always assuming, that is, that you would meet the sort of people you'd like to go out with anyway.'

Ron joined Dateline on the very same day as Fiona Martin, a pretty twenty-five-year-old from Penicuik, near Edinburgh. Widowed tragically young, Fiona had found it very difficult to get out to meet new people, especially as she had a small daughter. Fiona, like Ron, thought about Dateline for a long time – before being pushed into it by someone else, in her case her sister.

Fiona resolved to 'be very brave'.

Ron's name was on the first list of contacts Fiona received. She wrote back to three of the names, and went out with two.

'But they didn't really appeal to me. Then I met Ron.'

Before Ron had been sent his first list, he had a letter from Fiona. He wrote back, asking her to write or phone, and decided not to meet anyone else until he saw how things turned out with Fiona.

Impressed with his letter, Fiona resolved to 'be very brave' and ring Ron up. They arranged to meet.

Initially, that first encounter did not go particularly well. Ron picked Fiona up from her house and took her for a drink.

'I wasn't disappointed when I met her – I liked her,' Ron explained. 'But communication was very difficult because we were both nervous. I did most of the talking. I got the initial impression that she didn't like me very much.'

'And I didn't think he liked me either,' laughed Fiona.

By the time they were ready to go home, Ron had decided not to ask her for another date. But Scottish hospitality now made a fateful intervention – for Fiona invited him in for coffee and cheese toasties.

Once inside her own home, Ron immediately noticed, she became very much more confident and relaxed – 'and much easier to talk to'.

They sat and talked until after midnight.

'He ended up staying the night – on the couch.'

Fiona, too, saw Ron in a new light: 'I liked him very much,' she said. 'He ended up staying the night . . . On the couch downstairs,' she added hastily.

Ron was nevertheless still unconvinced that Fiona liked him, and was surprised and relieved the next morning when she agreed to go out with him a second time.

It was that second meeting that sealed it for Ron.

'It was when I was driving her home,' he remembered, 'that I suddenly realized I really wanted to make a go of this.'

Fiona too was beginning to feel that this was something special. 'I don't know why I was so attracted to him – it was just the sort of person he was. He's very kind and gentle.'

But Ron did not only have to convince Fiona. Jacqueline, her daughter, also had to be won over. It might not have been an easy matter for a single man with limited experience of children, but Ron proved to be a great success.

'Jacqueline took to him like . . . Well, put it this way: she can twist Ron round her little finger,' laughed Fiona.

'To be honest, I never really expected to meet a girl with a baby,' said Ron. 'But I must admit I greatly enjoy Jacqueline's company. It makes me feel . . . fulfilled.'

Five weeks after his and Fiona's first, nervous meeting, Ron warily broached the topic of marriage. He took the hypothetical route: 'If I were to ask you to marry me one day, what would you say?'

Fiona replied: 'I would think about for at least a second, and then say yes.'

'She just kissed me – and that was it.'

Ron waited another twenty-four hours before returning to the matter.

'I simply said, "How would it be if this time next year we were married?" She just kissed me, and that was it!'

After years of dithering – less than forty days of Dateline – Ron had finally found his bride.

Peter and Vicky

It was Vicky Jones's daughter who talked her into joining Dateline. Vicky, at forty-four, had been divorced seven years and had been spending progressively more time on her own.

'My daughter quite literally nagged me into joining,'

said Vicky. 'And when the first list of introductions arrived, she nagged me into contacting the people on it.'

Vicky's half-hearted attempts to make contacts were fruitless until, in the end – and as much to keep the peace as for any other reason – she told her daughter, 'You pick one out of the list and I'll phone him.'

The name was Peter Hunt. A forty-four-year-old factory supervisor from Horsham, West Sussex, Peter had been tragically widowed. He had remained alone for a time, but realized eventually that he must start meeting people again. His work provided no opportunities to meet eligible members of the opposite sex, and so he turned to Dateline.

'She nagged me into contacting the people.'

On the day Vicky rang, he was about to go out. Had she phoned any later, it is likely that she and Peter would never have met – so willing was Vicky to give up on any contact with whom she could not get in touch. 'I *have* phoned, but they're not in,' was Vicky's classic excuse to her daughter's persistent enquiries as to her progress with the list of names.

'Five minutes later and she would have missed me,' said Peter, who did not detect any reluctance in Vicky to talk once he had answered the phone.

'We spoke for about fifteen minutes,' he recollected, 'and then I rang back later and we were on the phone for about *two hours*. We talked and talked. At least *she* did,' he roared with laughter.

They arranged to meet, supposedly halfway between Horsham and Vicky's south London home.

39

'According to Vicky it was halfway, that is,' Peter recalled, laughing again at the memory. 'But it was about a mile away from her and forty miles from me!'

Peter was nevertheless looking forward to meeting Vicky. Her description of herself particularly intrigued him.

'You know that TV programme, *The Last of the Summer Wine?*' she had asked him on the phone. 'Well, I look a bit like Norah Batty.'

When they did meet – recognizing each other by the rather more dependable means of looking out for each other's cars in the parking area of their rendezvous, a pub – they were both nervous.

'I look a bit like Norah Batty.'

'I'd liked him from our phone talks,' Vicky recalled. 'But I didn't know what I really expected.'

But neither of them need have worried.

'After we started talking it was really just as it had been, chatting on the phone,' Peter said. 'It was natural. It felt right.'

Vicky quickly found things she liked about Peter.

'He had a warmth about him. It drew me to him,' she said, then added with a smile, 'I'm a chatterbox, and Peter's a very good listener.'

It was two weeks before they saw each other again, but from now on they spoke together on the phone every day.

'Don't ask me what we talked about,' laughed Vicky, 'but I do remember Peter's next phone bill was for more than £100!'

40

During their phone conversations, Vicky came to discover just how fond of Peter she was becoming. She had not realized how much so until in the midst of one call she surprised both Peter and herself by suggesting they should go away together for the coming Easter holiday.

'What are you doing for Easter?' she asked Peter.

'Well, nothing really.'

'Do you fancy going away for the weekend?'

Peter was momentarily lost for words – 'But I enjoyed her company, so I thought, why not?'

They decided on the West Country. When Peter turned up on Good Friday to collect her, Vicky had assembled most of her family to meet him.

'I wanted them to see who I was going away with,' she said.

'We were laughing all night long.'

It was on that day, according to Vicky, 'that I think I really and truly fell in love. But I was still worried we wouldn't get on, so I put £70 in my purse. At least I had my fare home!'

The weekend was one that neither of them will ever forget.

'The longer we were together, the more it seemed that was the way I wanted to carry on,' said Peter. 'By the Sunday, we had decided that we wanted to stay together.'

Peter asked her to marry him.

'It really threw me,' Vicky claimed.

She asked him to give her time to think about it –

and five minutes later she said "Yes, I'll marry you." '

'Then we couldn't stop laughing,' Vicky recalled. 'We were laughing all night long.'

Peter hoped Vicky would come to live at his Horsham home, but she told him again that she needed time to think about it. In the end, Peter came up to London to live with Vicky, selling his own home and commuting daily to work in Horsham.

'If that's not true love, you can't convince me of anything else!' declared Vicky.

The couple were married at Rotherhithe Register Office on the day chosen by Vicky, 22 June – three months to the day after their first meeting.

Vicky makes no secret of the fact that she met Peter through Dateline – in spite of her own slow start at making contact.

'My daughter certainly did the right thing by picking his name,' she said, acknowledging that the chance choice could just as easily have produced someone else. 'I was lucky, and I want to hang on to this one!'

4

Love at first sight

Dr. Robert Sharpe, of the Lifestyle Training Centre, writes: 'It ain't what you say, it's the way that you say it.'

It is an old adage, and none the less true for that. All of us, when going out on a first date, naturally worry about what to say to be interesting to the other party. But it is just as important to concentrate on giving the other person room to air their views. And there's no reason not to lapse into short silences from time to time so you can both enjoy the things around you – and to make yourself that much more attractive through 'body language'.

'Love at first sight' *is* a reality. So is its near relation, that sense of attraction which begins to mount in the first minutes of an encounter. But these miracles of magnetism are not simply magic; they comprise a complex jigsaw of different signals we send out to each other – many of them unconsciously.

Amongst these countless messages are those conveyed by good eye contact, confident posture (sitting or standing), smiling, demonstrating that you are listening attentively. Important, too, are the small, inoffensive touches which show that you feel close to someone without harassing them.

These are some of the ingredients in the stories of instant attraction described on the following pages.

Sally and Wally

'This man's a raving lunatic!' Sally Browning thought happily to herself as she read her first letter from Wally Gomes.

'There were reams of it – and I thought it was wonderful.'

Sally, twenty-six and a jewellery-shop manager in Truro, Cornwall, was new to Dateline. This was her first reply to the letters she had conscientiously written to all six of the names on her first contact list.

'They all wrote back – even two who were already seeing someone and simply wanted to wish me all the best,' said Sally. 'But Wally's letter was easily the most impressive one.'

While Sally had joined Dateline following the much-regretted end of a long relationship, Wally joined simply because he was relatively new to the West Country and hoped to find someone special. A native of Middlesbrough, Cleveland, he had gained his degree in Birmingham and now taught English in Plymouth, Devon.

'My friends were spread all over the country,' said Wally, thirty. 'I decided I wanted a closer relationship than anything I'd had to date.'

He and Sally exchanged three letters before Wally got around to putting his phone number down. But Sally was nervous of ringing.

'I just knew there was no way I was ever going to pluck up the courage to phone him,' she laughed. 'So I wrote back saying, "You will note my phone number is at the top of page one. If you wait for *me* to ring *you*, we'll both be drawing our pensions first!"'

Sally was sure he would ring as soon as he received the letter.

'I was like a cat on hot bricks all evening,' she remembered.

When the phone finally rang, Sally composed herself and answered it with the most sophisticated-sounding 'Hello' she could muster – only to find it was one of her female friends. When it rang again, she assumed it was the same friend calling back. She snatched up the receiver and snapped 'Yes?'

'Is that the old age pensioner in Truro?' enquired Wally.

'Yes, it is,' replied a convulsed Sally.

'I was like a cat on hot bricks all evening.'

'Well, here's the old bloke from Plymouth,' he announced.

That exchange launched an epic telephone conversation – lasting nearly two hours.

'We were both absolutely amazed at how well we got on,' said Wally. 'There was something that just clicked. We both felt it. Even during that first telephone call we were almost hinting that if we were to get together we would make a go of it.'

They arranged that Sally would take the coach to Plymouth, where Wally would meet her at the coach station.

'He said we each ought to wear a pink carnation and carry a rolled-up newspaper,' Sally laughed. 'But I said no, I wouldn't come! We compromised on carrying flowers, and exchanging photographs.'

So it was that a month after she had first written to Wally, Sally found herself Plymouth-bound – clutching a bunch of enormous daisies.

'The coach was early and he was late, and it was freezing cold,' she recalled. 'I arrived about 9 pm, and there are some pretty funny types hanging about the bus station at that time of night, I can tell you! So there I sat in the bitter cold with my knees shaking and holding on to my daisies – which were wilting by now – for dear life. I just couldn't stop my knees shaking, and I couldn't make up my mind whether it was nerves or the cold.'

Wally had told her that he would be wearing white jeans and sneakers.

'I thought, *I could get to like you.*'

'So every bloke that went past – I was looking at his legs!'

But Wally spotted Sally first.

'It was the daisies. She always doodled daisies on her letters.'

'Wally was tons better than his photo,' Sally remembered thinking. 'I looked at him and thought, "I could get to like you".'

He took her home to a hot meal. Knowing she was a vegetarian – they both are now – Wally served up a quiche. But neither was especially interested in eating.

46

They talked, they listened to records. And they fell in love.

'It was, definitely, love at first sight for both of us,' Wally states firmly. 'In fact, it was love at first letter!'

Sally stayed the weekend.

'We were so comfortable with each other that we started to talk about domestic things. We seemed just to take it for granted we would be sharing our lives.'

Wally proposed to Sally on the Sunday.

'I'm going to ask you a question and I want you to promise you'll say yes.'

Sally made her promise – and kept it.

'I certainly didn't think it would happen on the first meeting,' Sally admitted. 'The first person I wrote to and the first person I met. But that was it. I wouldn't find anyone I liked better than him.'

'I couldn't otherwise see any way of meeting somebody.'

Sally agreed that the decision to get married might have seemed a hasty one.

'But I am a very careful person,' she insisted. 'I had been hurt in the past and I wasn't about to let myself get hurt again. I don't know what it is with Wally but he just came over as someone I could entrust with my emotions. He just bowled me over completely.'

Wally and Sally were married five months later at St Peter's Catholic Church in Plymouth.

'Really it was one of those cases where you think, let's just go away and get married straightaway,' said

Wally. 'And but for our two mothers we would have done that.'

Sally's mother – at whose insistence Sally had joined Dateline in the first place – was delighted with her wedding plans, and thought her new son-in-law wonderful.

'I can stop worrying about you now,' she told Sally.

Sally has no illusions as to how much of a part Dateline has played in her happiness.

'Looking at it logically, and particularly in my age group, I couldn't otherwise see any way of meeting somebody. I don't like pubs and clubs – and the sort of people you meet in them are not interested in the things that interest me, such as animals and the countryside. If someone's in the same situation and, like me, they don't like leaving things to chance, I'd recommend them to do as I have done.'

Wally is equally enthusiastic.

'Everything has turned out just as I wanted; it's all fallen into place. Sally's changed my life completely.'

Alison and Philip

In 1982, Philip Wentworth's life seemed in ruins. Badly injured in a motorcycle accident, he was off work for many months. Then his marriage broke up. Finally, he was made redundant.

But Philip fought back. Aged twenty-nine, he set up as a self-employed musician – and found plenty of work in and around his home town of Cinderford in Gloucestershire. As things improved, he began to turn his mind to finding someone to share his life with again.

It was a Dateline advertisement in a Sunday paper that set him thinking he had been on his own quite long enough. *Find your ideal woman*, it said. The phrase stuck in his mind.

'I wasn't in any hurry to get married again,' Philip recalled. 'But I thought it would be nice to make some new female friends.'

When he joined Dateline, one of the first two names sent to Philip was that of Alison Lewis, of Portishead near Bristol. He wrote to her, with a note of his telephone number.

'I was fascinated by his voice. It was lovely!'

Alison duly rang him, but three times got his answering machine.

A twenty-five-year-old nursery assistant, Alison had been a Dateline member nearly a year, and had been in two minds about ringing Philip at all. She was close to giving up her search for what she freely admitted was 'somebody to fall in love with'.

But she refused, nevertheless, to be deterred by the answering machine – upon which she was unable to leave a message for Philip to call her back, as she had no phone of her own. Disembodied as Philip's message on the machine was, Alison had to confess that 'I was fascinated by his voice. It was lovely!'

So on that third encounter with the machine, Alison left a message that she would call back at a specific time the same evening. Philip got the message – and stayed in.

When the call came, they spoke together for three-quarters of an hour. Philip asked Alison for the call-box number and rang back, and they would have talked even longer, Alison said, if it had not been for a stormy-faced woman waiting her turn . . .

They arranged to meet on the following Thursday. He picked her up from her home for a day out at Weston-super-Mare. Alison had been waiting for him anxiously, and rushed out to meet him as soon as she saw him get out of his car.

Philip recalled that she was not as he had pictured her. He thought she would be taller than her five-foot-four, and would have a different hairstyle.

'The burning question is, do you want to see me again?'

'I was a bit cautious,' he admitted, referring obliquely back to his unhappy past. 'But once we got chatting there were no problems at all. I found her easy to talk to.'

Alison had no reservations at all.

'It was love at first sight,' she said breathlessly. 'That's the only way I can describe it. He was just wonderful – a gentleman.'

One particular thing about Philip made an immediate impression on her.

'I was brought up to shake hands when you meet people. With most of the guys I dated I would hold my hand out and say, "Hi. I'm Alison." And they would always hesitate. This time I decided I would not hold my hand out, I'll just say hello and be myself. But Phil held out *his* hand to *me*.'

They had a memorable day together.

'Phil was nervous, I could sense that,' Alison remembered. 'But as the day passed he relaxed more and more. It was wonderful. We walked and talked, had lunch, held hands. Even the weather was glorious!'

When Philip took her home, Alison invited him in to meet her parents. Before he left, the couple sat in his car briefly.

'Well,' said Philip anxiously. 'The burning question is, do you want to see me again?'

'Oh, yes please,' came the fervent reply.

'It blossomed from that moment,' Philip recollected.

'She came over as, literally, my ideal woman.'

They were apart during the following week as Philip had a family commitment in Hastings. To Alison, it seemed like for ever, but she was buoyed up by a letter from Philip.

'He was missing me. He saw young couples holding hands, and told me how he wished I was with him in Hastings. It really pleased me.'

When they were reunited, Philip found that all his initial cautiousness had vanished – swallowed up in the warmth of Alison's feelings for him.

'We did a lot of talking,' he remembered. 'You can usually tell whether someone's genuine or not. In that respect she came over as, literally, my ideal woman.'

The couple were finding it increasingly difficult to say goodnight to one another. Their evenings together became later and later. One such night, they were at Alison's home in the living room in the small hours: 'We were doing what young lovers do, and talking, and all of a sudden there was silence,' Alison recalled with a smile. 'As we were kissing, Phil pulled gently away from me and said, "Ali, will you marry me?" It was beautiful. Really lovely. I said, "Will you say that again?" He did, and I felt myself saying "Yes, yes, yes, please".'

The birds were beginning to sing as Philip finally made his way home.

Alison and Philip were married at the Methodist Church in Portishead eight months after they first met. Their happiness has since been made complete by the arrival of a daughter, Katie Louise.

Julie and Kerry

Weightlifting, confessed twenty-six-year-old Kerry Stone, occupied a higher place on his list of priorities than meeting women at the time he joined Dateline. A warehouse storeman from Swindon, Wiltshire, Kerry had filled his life with training and hobbies since being divorced, and was persuaded to join Dateline by a neighbour.

'He had joined three or four different kinds of dating agencies, and he used to keep on and on at me. It was when I was browsing through a magazine and saw a Dateline advertisement that I thought I might as well have a go.'

But even when Kerry received his first set of six introductions, he was still lukewarm about the idea. He didn't meet any of the girls, despite writing to most of them.

Things did start to happen – slowly – with the second lot. Kerry made contact by telephone this time, and dated several girls. He was on his fourth list when he encountered the name of Julie Shepherd, from Bath.

Kerry was one of Julie's first Dateline contacts. Single and twenty-four, Julie had found that her arduous job as a hospital ward sister made it hard to summon up the energy to get out and meet people after work. As for eligible doctors at her hospital, there simply weren't any.

Three of the people given Julie's name telephoned her on the same evening.

'So I arranged to meet them the following weekend – Friday, Saturday and Sunday!' said Julie.

Kerry was the Saturday date. Friday's had not been a success, so it was with mixed feelings that Julie opened the door to Kerry.

Kerry hadn't had an ideal start to the evening, having found that Julie's home was on one of Bath's famous steep hills, and that the handbrake on his car was not up to the job. His attempts to park were consequently something of a spectacle.

'Oh! He's rather nice.'

'She must have been looking out of the window, thinking what an awful driver I was,' laughed Kerry.

What Julie actually thought when she saw him was, 'Oh! He's rather nice.'

That first date was a complete success, if a rather hectic one.

'We went to about eight pubs,' said Julie. 'Kerry's friends had recommended quite a number in Bath, and he was determined to try them all.'

Kerry and Julie none the less had plenty of time to get acquainted.

'Really, on that first date, well – that was it for me,' remembered Julie. 'We just got on so well. Apart, that is, from one point where he thought I'd run out on him. I went to the Ladies in one pub and he said I was gone for what seemed like hours. He thought I'd escaped through the window!'

Kerry was anxious indeed not to lose sight of her.

'I was shell-shocked that I got on with her so well. She had an outlook that was different to anybody else.'

At the end of the evening, Kerry agreed to phone Julie on the following Wednesday and they would 'take it from there'.

Julie found herself fervently hoping he would ring. She cancelled her Sunday-night date.

'If I'd told people I wanted to marry her after a week they'd think I was crazy.'

Kerry called as promised, and they started meeting almost every night – in spite of Kerry having to drive more than thirty miles from Swindon each time, and having to be at work by 8 am each morning.

Within a week, although nothing was said, they both knew they were in love.

'If I'd told people I wanted to marry her after a week, they would think I was crazy,' said Kerry. 'But that was what happened.'

It was Julie's birthday the following weekend. Kerry joined her – and twenty-five workmates – for a celebration picnic in Bath's Royal Crescent, alongside the crowds assembled for the start of the city's arts festival.

Julie is certain that it was on this happy occasion that Kerry decided how he felt about her.

'I was just waiting for the proposal,' she recalled with a laugh. Julie, as Kerry had discovered to his pleasure by now, is a lady who laughs a lot.

But she had to wait another week for the proposal. They had planned to go away for a day together on the May bank holiday Monday – and Kerry had intended to propose then.

'But I couldn't wait,' Kerry admitted. 'When I got down to Bath on the Friday I came out with it.'

Julie elaborated: 'He said, "I think I'd quite like to marry you". I said, "What do you mean 'quite like'? Do you want to or not?" Then he said, "Well yes, I think so". And that was it.'

'I really didn't think about marrying anyone.'

The couple's bank holiday plans were abandoned in favour of a rapid visit to Julie's parents in Derbyshire.

'I actually asked her dad if I could marry Julie,' said Kerry. 'He seemed quite chuffed when I asked him.'

'My mum was speechless at first,' Julie remembered. 'But then she just said "Oh. Right then."'

Kerry's parents were equally bemused when the couple called on them on their way back from Derbyshire.

'They were having their kitchen renovated, and the place was a real mess,' said Kerry. 'But they liked Julie then, and they like her now.'

*

Julie's parents were not to learn until some months later that the couple had met through Dateline. Kerry, however, had told his parents beforehand. His mother had merely laughed, and his father had told him he thought he was stupid. Delighted with his daughter-in-law, his father no longer holds that view!

Kerry and Julie were married at the Register Office in Bath a year after their first meeting. The marriage was blessed in the chapel of Julie's hospital. Earlier in that week the couple had had an unexpected experience – appearing on television.

'It was the TV-AM "Spring Brides" feature,' explained Julie. 'I think they picked us because we were a bit different, having met through computer dating.'

For Julie, the whole experience of meeting Kerry and starting married life had been an unexpected one.

'I joined Dateline because I thought I'd probably meet lots of people,' she admitted with her characteristic laughter. 'I really didn't think about marrying anyone!'

Chris and Julie

'She was horrible to me!'

That's how twenty-three-year-old Chris Healey summed up his first encounter with the woman to whom he is now married, Julie.

Chris, a postman from Dukinfield, Cheshire, had telephoned Julie on a Saturday morning, as soon as he received his first list of Dateline contacts.

Julie, twenty-one, had to admit it: 'I was really awful to him,' she said, blushing. 'I don't know why.'

Julie had already met five young men through Dateline. She agreed that she may have been offhand with the luckless Chris because she had not particularly liked any of her previous contacts. She didn't feel like making the effort to meet him.

Julie's brusque manner left Chris tongue-tied, and while he was wondering what to say next, she solved it for him.

'This is a bit stupid,' she said. 'Write me a letter and send me a photograph and I'll get in touch with you.'

'He had a really, really soft voice.'

Chris, undaunted, did just that.

Julie, in the mean time, found herself thinking often about that phone call, and about Chris.

'I liked the sound of him on the phone,' she recalled. 'He had a really, really soft voice.'

The next time they spoke was to arrange to meet – outside the Electricity Board showroom in Darwen, Julie's home town in Lancashire.

It might not have seemed the most likely place for a young couple to fall in love, but according to Julie, that's exactly what happened.

'As soon as I saw him, I thought, "Well, this is the one" – and it was!' she remembered.

Chris felt much the same. 'As soon as I saw her, I just fell for her. When she started to talk, I couldn't believe this was the same person who had been so nasty to me on the phone.'

They talked the evening away in a pub, then moved on to Julie's home for coffee; Chris reluctantly tore himself away at 3 am.

'I had to be at work at 5 o'clock!' he said, laughing. 'I don't know how I kept awake.'

The couple had arranged to meet again in Blackpool, where Julie was about to start a week's holiday. So their second encounter consisted of a Sunday afternoon with Julie's family, then a quiet meal to-

---

'I didn't have a lot of sleep that week.'

---

gether – and another early-hours departure for his 5 am start for Chris.

'I didn't have a lot of sleep that week!'

Chris returned to Blackpool on Wednesday, as soon as he had finished work.

By 2.15 that afternoon, the couple were engaged. Julie accepted Chris's proposal immediately.

'He asked Julie why someone as nice as her had to join Dateline.'

'She wasn't surprised,' said Chris. 'I know she had an idea what I was going to say, because when I said, "Can I ask you something?", she had a look in her eyes as though she was certain what the question would be.'

Julie's mother, who had paid for her daughter to join Dateline in the first place, was nevertheless rather dazed at the speed of events – Julie engaged to a man she had first met only five days previously.

'Are you sure?' was her first, incredulous question.

Chris's parents were delighted at the news.

58

'Dad was over the moon,' said Chris. 'He asked Julie why somebody as nice as her had to join Dateline!'

Julie and Chris were married in Darwen five months after their first meeting. Julie, radiant in white, was attended by four bridesmaids and a page-boy – plus 120 guests.

Chris managed to transfer his work to Darwen, and the couple now have their own home in the town. Chris is happy indeed to have been undeterred by that first, inauspicious encounter with Julie on the telephone: 'I knew she was right for me.'

Phyllis and Tony

Tony Whitehead's Dateline membership got off to a slow start. A forty-five-year-old stock controller from north London, Tony joined because he had been divorced four years, and was tired of being alone.

In his first six months with Dateline, he received seventeen introductions – and only met one of them.

'Every time I rang someone up there was nobody at home,' said Tony.

Then one Saturday morning *his* phone rang. It was Phyllis Stevens. She explained that Dateline had given her his name. She was a new member, and Tony was only the second man she had contacted; she had arranged a meeting with the first for the following Monday.

Phyllis, a widow of forty-four who had been eagerly encouraged by her children – all six of them – to rebuild her social life, invited Tony to come and see her that very evening.

When he arrived at her south London home, Phyllis's

niece let Tony in. As soon as the couple met, their mutual attraction was immediately obvious to both of them.

'I don't know why,' recalled Phyllis, 'but something there just clicked.'

'It was just something that happened between us,' said Tony. 'It was just one of those things. I knew she was the person for me.'

'Something there just clicked.'

They did not go out, partly because Phyllis was recovering from a recent illness. They simply spent a cosy, companionable evening together – during which Phyllis found herself hoping very much that Tony would ask to see her again.

He did – for the following day.

Phyllis asked Tony to come for lunch, and they found themselves again completely at home in each other's company. By the evening, their conversation had come around to the topic of whether or not either of them would marry again. Immediately after Tony had said that he definitely would, he took a deep breath, looked Phyllis intently in the eye and asked: 'Would you marry me?'

'Yes,' she replied.

They both swear that it was as simple as that.

'I knew he was the man for me,' said Phyllis, echoing Tony's own words. 'I don't know why. I just did. I just knew he was meant for me.'

The following day, the couple went out together to buy the rings. And Phyllis had a phone call to make –

to tell the one other Dateline member she had contacted that she would not be keeping the date they had made for that day.

Phyllis and Tony were married two months later at Wandsworth Town Hall in south London. Their respective families were delighted for them.

'I just knew he was meant for me.'

Tony admits to being still a little dazed at his good fortune, but is very, very happy with his new life. He has no qualms about having enlisted the aid of a computer in the quest for his perfect partner: 'It's a wonderful way of meeting the right person.'

5

Country life – and moving experiences

For many single people, problems in finding partners are simply the product of geography. Too many of us chasing too few jobs means an increased mobility of labour in Britain. That in its turn means more of us relocating to places where we are complete strangers – particularly to other single people.

And then there are the difficulties encountered by single people living in sparsely populated areas. Country life is, of course, the dream of many (particularly of those who live in crowded cities and view the rural existence through rose-tinted spectacles!), but one of its realities is a distinctly diminished range of opportunities for encountering the opposite sex.

Dateline's nationwide service is consequently especially valuable to these two groups of people – as some of the experiences in this chapter reveal.

Gary and Lorraine

Moving from Glasgow to the other end of Britain – Portsmouth in Hampshire – meant Gary Cox found himself a complete stranger to his new home town. He had been married before, and particularly missed the company of a special woman in his life.

'I joined Dateline purely on the basis that I wanted to meet a few people,' said Gary, twenty-three.

Lorraine Gattrell, from the village of Lavant near Chichester, was experiencing similar problems in meeting people.

'I was working as a nanny and stuck in a house with three children,' said nineteen-year-old Lorraine. 'I didn't get out very much.'

She found the courage, after much heart-searching, to join Dateline – but then put off contacting any of the people on her first list of names for six months. That was the time it took her to write to Gary.

'I didn't get out very much.'

In the mean time, Lorraine had met a number of the young men to whom her name had been sent. Gary, too, in a year with Dateline, had seen several of his contacts. Neither of them had thus far formed any serious attachments.

The arrival of Lorraine's letter coincided with another, Gary remembered: 'I'd been away on business, and came back to find a pile of letters. One was from a girlfriend who I had been out with, saying that she didn't want to see me any more.'

But Gary was determined not to be discouraged by such news. He looked on the bright side, and took up the suggestion Lorraine had made in her letter that he should ring her up.

Lorraine spent much of that first – and rather lengthy – telephone chat laughing; she was much taken with Gary's irresistible sense of humour, and excitedly anticipated the meeting they arranged.

Both of them were immediately impressed with one another when they met. Each told the other all about themselves, although Gary did conceal the fact that he had been previously married.

'I didn't want to bring it up on that first night,' he recalled. 'I was afraid it might spoil things if I wanted to see her again.'

'I think he expected me to turn round and walk off.'

Although their second meeting was another very happy one, in which they spoke frankly about their feelings for each other, Gary again did not reveal his secret to Lorraine. He was still, understandably, afraid to break the spell that had been cast between them.

Three weeks – and many more happy encounters – after their first meeting, Gary finally cleared the air. He made a real day of it.

First, he introduced Lorraine to his parents. That evening, the couple had a meal together – and Gary told her about his previous marriage.

'I think he expected me to turn round and walk off,' Lorraine recalled. 'I admit it was a bit of a shock, but actually I told him it didn't matter.'

Lorraine also felt that Gary, having had a failed marriage, would be that much more careful to avoid making the same kind of mistake again.

Hugely relieved and happy at the way Lorraine had reacted, Gary now had another surprise to spring on her. They had arranged to go to a nightclub that night – and it was there, amidst the hubbub, that Gary quite suddenly asked Lorraine to marry him.

She thought he must be joking.

'Are you serious?' she asked.

'Yes,' he replied simply.

'"Are you serious?" she asked.'

She could see that indeed he was – and she knew she felt the same.

Gary and Lorraine waited almost a year before getting married. Speedy as the engagement had been, they had plenty of time to learn about each other before the ceremony – which was held at Chichester Register Office, followed by a blessing in the parish church at Lavant.

Until the wedding, the couple were in the habit of telling their friends that they had met in a nightclub. At their reception on the great day, however, Gary's best man made sure that that was one secret the groom would no longer be able to keep to himself . . .

James and June

At thirty, James Munro took stock of his single life. Earlier relationships had all ended, and he had lately been giving more attention to his work – as an oil-industry administrator – than to his emotional life.

Meeting girls, James had to admit to himself, was a

bit of a problem, since he had to spend a lot of his time away from his Aberdeen home – on a North Sea oil platform. So James joined Dateline.

Twenty-seven-year-old June Black, meanwhile, had resolved to do the same. A long-standing relationship had recently ended for her; her girlfriends were all married; her job in a supermarket in her home town of Peterhead – twenty miles north of Aberdeen – did not give her contact with eligible men. On top of it all, she was simply very lonely.

James was nearing the end of his first year's membership when his name was sent to June on her first list of contacts. A lively correspondence grew up between the two of them. They were in no rush to meet, particularly as they were in the middle of a typically hard Highland winter which made travel treacherous. James's work was keeping him off-shore much of the time, too. Their friendship built up steadily through letters and the photographs they exchanged.

'I was keen on him in a funny sort of way.'

June, in the mean time, did not request any more names from Dateline.

'I did think there could be a future for us,' she said. 'I was quite comfortable getting to know James through his letters. I was keen on him in a funny sort of way . . .'

Then one day in the spring, June's phone rang. It was James.

'After writing for so long, it was strange to suddenly hear his voice,' June remembered.

They agreed to meet at a petrol station in Peterhead's outskirts. Not the most romantic rendezvous, but preferable to the strong likelihood that James would otherwise get irretrievably lost in the bewildering maze that is Peterhead's town centre.

James's first sight of June delighted him.

'I thought immediately how much better-looking she was than in her photograph. How nice she was to look at, to speak to – the sound of her voice.'

'I was taken aback at first,' June remembered. 'Seeing him in person was totally different from his photo. I liked what I saw in the person more than I'd seen from his picture.'

They had a meal together – and thoroughly enjoyed themselves.

'Everything was just so lovely,' said James. 'We talked non-stop.'

**'I leaned across to kiss her goodnight, and
we were still there an hour later.'**

At the end of the evening he drove June back to the home she shared with her parents.

'I leaned across the car to kiss her goodnight, and we were still there an hour later!'

Driving home, James couldn't have been more elated. He had waited a long time for someone like June.

Their next date took them to Inverness for a picnic on an idyllic spring day. A perfect day, in fact, for falling in love, made all the more memorable by the heart-shaped earrings James bought for June in the town, and which she has worn constantly ever since.

From that day, June said, 'I just felt in my mind that he was the one I wanted.'

They began to see each other more and more often, and to talk in earnest about the prospect of marriage. But James did his best to keep his feet on the ground. His contract at work was due for renewal, and he felt he should have this confirmed before getting formally engaged.

Then, in August, while James was working off-shore, June had to go into hospital for a foot operation. James wrote to her there, and told her he had a surprise in store. He would be visiting as soon as he came ashore.

It was evening before he made it to the hospital – a little early for visiting time, so he had to wait outside the ward. June's fellow patients could see him and told her excitedly, 'He's here! He's here!'

'I'd not a clue what to say to her.'

June herself was immobile. Her foot was heavily plastered, confining her to bed, where she was surrounded by the flowers James had had sent in while he was off-shore.

Now he could come in, and he walked straight to her bed, kissed her and presented her with a bottle of her favourite perfume. As a thrilled June was examining the gift, James took her left hand and gently drew it towards him. Without a word, he slipped a beautiful sapphire and diamond ring on to her third finger.

'I'd not a clue what to say to her,' he remembered with a smile, 'so I simply put the ring on!'

68

The news telegraphed around the ward at astounding speed.

'I looked up and there were smiling faces everywhere,' said James.

Nurses now materialized from all directions to offer congratulations, and with them came a trolley loaded with glasses and sherry. The good news had clearly been anticipated.

June was already on the telephone to her mother with the glad tidings. It was an unforgettably happy evening for the couple – and it certainly did wonders for the morale of every patient in the ward . . .

James and June plan to marry in early summer, one year after their first meeting in that petrol station outside Peterhead. June will be moving to Aberdeen.

'My life has changed completely since I met James,' she says. 'In fact, I don't know what my life was without him.'

Fiona and Robert

Two years working in Australia meant that Robert Warner lost contact with many of the people he had known in his native Leicester. He came home to find that most of his friends were by now married. His new job, as a machine-tool fitter, was a good one – but it hardly brought him into everyday contact with eligible girls.

Robert, aged thirty, had his own house in Leicester, and a growing dislike of the single life. He made up his mind to join Dateline. His resolve to join, however, failed to extend as far as actually making contact with the young women whose names he was sent. Although he received seventeen introductions in all, he just could not summon up the nerve to get in touch with any of them.

But all was not lost. Robert's name was sent to a number of women, and one who contacted him was twenty-five-year-old Fiona Morris. A newcomer to Dateline, she had picked Robert from her first list of six names by a less than scientific method.

'I just closed my eyes and stabbed a pin into the list.'

'I just closed my eyes and stabbed a pin into the list,' recalled Fiona. 'Robert's name was the one, and I decided to ring him.'

In the hour-long call, a hesitant start led on to an arrangement to meet at Fiona's home.

Robert's first impression of Fiona as she opened the door to him on their first encounter was a memorably good one.

'She's got big, dark brown eyes,' was the first thing that really struck him about her. And he can remember liking her immediately.

Their date – which consisted simply of a sortie to the pub – was a resounding success. They got on so well together that Robert found himself promising to ring the next day to arrange another meeting; his initial nerves were soon forgotten.

He did phone Fiona the next day, and they arranged to meet the same evening. Robert was anxious to see her again: 'I just wanted to make sure that my first impressions were right,' he recalled with a smile.

Fiona's feelings about Robert were no less enthusiastic: 'From the beginning I thought he was special,' she said.

Even after just those first two dates, Fiona candidly admitted, 'I got the feeling that he was the one for me, and I was hoping that it would come to marriage.'

It was shortly before Easter, just a few weeks after they had first met, that Robert appeared on Fiona's doorstep bearing a bunch of flowers. He had made up his mind to propose.

'From the beginning I thought he was special.'

They went out for a meal, and Robert did his best to steer the conversation round to the topic of marriage. Fiona didn't give him any clear signals as to whether she would say yes or no, and it was not until they were back at her house having coffee that Robert finally took the plunge.

They were sitting together on the sofa when he slid down on to his knees and asked her.

To his huge delight – not to mention relief – Fiona said 'yes' immediately.

They were married at the village church in Branston near Lincoln in May, just ten weeks and two days after they first met.

Lynn and Mark

'I was wanting to get married: I was looking for the perfect wife.'

That was the single reason – admitted with disarming frankness – why twenty-three-year-old Mark Slater from Alness in the Scottish Highlands joined Dateline.

So keen was he to find absolutely the right person that he made no limit to the parts of the UK from which the computer could make selections. *Who* was very much more important to him than *where*.

Initial contact was necessarily by letter, and one of the girls with whom Mark corresponded seemed very soon to stand out from the rest. She was Lynn Overton, just eighteen, from Mablethorpe in Lincolnshire – 400 miles to the south.

'I was looking for a husband.'

Lynn, too, was frank about her reasons for joining Dateline: 'I was looking for a husband. Someone special I could settle down with. I'd had a few boyfriends, but none of them was suitable.'

Lynn and Mark exchanged letters for two months; they sent each other photographs. A serious relationship began to form.

They agreed that Mark should travel to Mablethorpe. Lynn recognized him at once when she spotted him at the station.

'She put her arm around me and gave me a big hug,' Mark recalled happily.

He stayed with Lynn and her family for two weeks. In that time, the couple's feelings for each other turned into love.

'By the end of those weeks I had decided that he was the one,' said Lynn firmly.

72

So sure was she that she decided not to let Mark go home to Scotland without her. So he returned to Alness with Lynn beside him.

With plans to marry later in the year, Lynn is currently staying with Mark and his family. Neither of the couple feels they are too young to settle down to married life.

'She put her arms round me and give me a big hug.'

Mark grins cheerfully: 'I'd always pictured myself coming home from work and my wife cooking my tea – and giving me a kiss by the cooker,' he said, maintaining the straightest face he could manage amidst the shrieks of laughter from Lynn and his mother.

Ann and Steven

Steven Pyne grew up in Devon but moved away after school, finally returning to live in Plympton when he was twenty-nine. He found, naturally, that most of the friends of his teenage years had in the mean time married and settled down. Without a girlfriend, or much prospect of finding one, Steven considered Dateline – and took the plunge.

'I met the first one – a definite non-starter!' laughed Steve. 'But they steadily improved. I met a couple that were fairly long-standing. Then Ann came along.'

By now, Steve had been a Dateline member for a year, and Ann for just a week. She, too, had lived away from home for some years, but had now moved to Torquay to be with her parents. At twenty-seven, and working as a secretary at Television South West in Plymouth, Ann was meeting a lot of women, but had little male contact.

'I had had boyfriends, but nothing that was permanent. I thought Dateline would be a good way of getting to know men, even if it didn't mean having them as long-term boyfriends.'

In fact, it was Ann's mother who finally convinced her to join Dateline, because Ann seemed to be spending too much time at home. 'She was more worried about my future than I was!' recalls Ann.

'Not bad,' he thought. 'Definitely worth following up.'

Steve initially contacted Ann by letter. She wrote back, with a photograph.

'Not bad,' Steve remembers thinking. 'Definitely worth following up.'

To Steve's next letter Ann responded with her phone number.

'I plucked up the courage to ring her. I don't like using the telephone really, but we hit if off straight-away.'

Steve's first letter had impressed Ann.

'It was very chatty, one of the best I'd received. He had been on Dateline quite a while and knew what to put in and what to leave out.'

Ann did sense Steve's dislike of the telephone.

'That first conversation was a bit stilted,' she said.

'But we chat for ever on the phone now. We can't get off it!'

They agreed to meet outside the Princess Theatre in Torquay. From her photograph, Steve soon recognized Ann, but he hesitated to approach.

'Is this her?' he thought to himself, as much out of playing for time as from any real doubt.

Finally, he walked up to her.

'Are you Ann?' he asked.

'He was obviously nervous,' recalled Ann. 'We both were. But I liked him from the first.'

They set off – 'at a cracking pace', Ann remembers – to the nearest pub.

'We just sat and chatted all evening,' said Ann. 'He really seemed right from the start, whereas the others I'd actually met were a bit awkward. With Steve, it just seemed right.'

'He was obviously nervous. We both were.'

Steve felt the same way.

'That first date went very well. It didn't seem to last all that long, for one thing. It went so quickly.'

Steve was in no doubt that he wanted to see Ann again, and Ann was happy to agree. They met again the very next night.

'The attraction was fairly instant,' Steve confessed. 'I'd not had that feeling to that extent before. Some of the others were a little bit, well, rural. They were nice people,' he added, hastily, 'but not quite the same as me. Whereas Ann shares my background, having moved around a bit.'

A week after they first met, Steve sent Ann a dozen red roses. It was a particularly timely gesture, as Ann had been feeling low following her mother's admission to hospital.

The couple began to date every week – and their relationship deepened.

But Steve had no cause for complacency. Shortly after their first meeting, Ann did go out with another Dateline member. When she told Steve about this, he was very upset. It was a reaction that set Ann to thinking.

'I knew it wasn't fair to Steve,' said Ann. 'I had to stop this and go out only with Steve. I felt he was special. It seemed good from the start, but realizing I was in love took time – maybe two months.

'I'm certainly glad I persevered.'

'We shared so much in common. There was something there I'd never known with boyfriends I'd had before. He is very considerate. That's something I noticed from the start. Other fellows tended to be very egotistical, a bit macho. That really irritates me. They seem to want you to be their possession. But Steve's not like that at all.'

'I was thinking about Ann all the time,' said Steve.

He put his dislike of the telephone firmly behind him: 'I kept ringing up just to chat inanely. With the others, it had been a chore to ring them up for a date.'

Ann and Steve became engaged after six months. He had actually proposed some weeks earlier – almost unintentionally.

'I was buying my own house, and I thought how silly it was not to have anybody to share it with,' explained Steve. 'We were having coffee at Ann's parents' place, and I just asked her – somewhat hopefully – if she would like to get married.'

'It came as a bit of a shock,' Ann recalls, 'even though it had been in the air for a while. I wanted to think about it. So I thought about it for a week – and then said yes.'

Steve and Ann plan to marry next year, eighteen months after the Dateline computer matched them.

'I've told most of my friends how Steve and I met,' said Ann, 'and some of them have since told me they have friends in Dateline and it's worked for them too. There's no stigma attached to it. I don't know why everyone doesn't tell others about it. It's just a way of meeting people.'

Steve admitted to having had his doubts at one stage.

'On one list I only got one introduction, and another person I wrote to replied that she was getting married. But I'm certainly glad that I persevered.'

6

Starting over – after divorce

The unhappy statistic that one in three marriages ends in divorce is an oft-quoted one. But as every couple who have been through the experience know, the bitter end of a once-sweet romance means that life is never the same again. The fact that the experience is so common is little, if any, consolation.

A particular poignant consequence of the high level of marriage breakdowns is that there are now a million lone-parent families in Britain. That means that one in every seven households with dependent children is headed by a single parent.

Christine Orton, of the lone-parent organization Gingerbread, has this to say.

It's not an easy job bringing up children alone. The dual task of caring for home and family and finding an income must be done by one person. And for a great many divorced, separated and unmarried lone parents, this is not by choice, but by force of circumstance.

These families have some problems in common:
Isolation Without the companionship of a partner, many single parents experience great loneliness. Particularly when their children are young, they may find it difficult to get out to meet new friends. There is no

78

one to share worries – or decisions – with, no one to give comfort when things go wrong.

Lack of support All the thousand-and-one practical tasks of everyday life must be done alone – from jobs around the home to paying bills, to fixing up holidays. For the divorced person there may be added problems over access to children.

Low income Because daycare provision in Britain is so scarce, a large proportion of lone parents are unable to work. They must rely instead on welfare benefits – and on a single income many live below the poverty line.

On top of these problems, lone parents are often the target of thoughtless criticism. They are labelled as scroungers living off the state, or as irresponsible people just out for a good time. There have been accusations that without the care of two parents, children are destined to grow up into juvenile delinquents and disturbed adults.

But just because one-parent families have problems, they do not have to be 'problem families'. The majority cope amazingly well under very difficult circumstances, particularly when they are given the right support.

Gingerbread operates through 300 local self-help groups in England and Wales.

It is all intended to help lone parents feel less alone, better able to manage problems as they arise, and, if they want to, to find new relationships and happiness.

Margaret and Michael

'I was doing very, very little with my life. It virtually revolved around my daughter.'

79

That's how thirty-eight-year-old maintenance supervisor Michael Wells recalled the time before he met his new fiancée, Margaret Johnson. Divorced two years and living with fifteen-year-old Julie in his home in Solihull, Warwickshire, Michael joined Dateline in the hope of finding someone to settle down with. He had always considered himself a family man by instinct. Inevitable as he had realized his divorce was, it had still made him very unhappy and despondent about a life alone.

Margaret, thirty-six, had herself been divorced – nine years previously. She had struggled bravely for all that time to bring up her two children – Karen, fifteen, and John, twelve – in her Nuneaton council house.

Joining Dateline was a serious decision for her, from the financial point of view among others. 'Being a single parent, I don't have much money, so I had to save up for a while,' she said.

'He was exactly how I'd thought he would be.'

Margaret dated a few of the men whose names she received, but it was to be five months before she met the man with the right 'chemistry' for her.

From a list of six names, Michael decided, for some reason he still cannot explain, just to write to Margaret. He waited anxiously for her reply – which duly came, complete with her telephone number. They arranged by phone to meet on the following Monday, in the Nuneaton station car park.

'I was an hour early,' Michael remembered with a grin. 'I had given Margaret the registration number of my car for recognition; I described it to her, too, as two-tone – blue and rust!'

She spotted him without problem.

'From his voice and his letter I'd built up this picture in my mind of what he would be like,' said Margaret. 'And he was exactly how I'd thought he would be.'

They spent an hour strolling around the Nuneaton shops, talking easily to one another. Margaret was filled with excited hope.

'I described the car to her as two-tone: blue and rust.'

'This time the chemistry was there,' she said.

She invited him to her home for the afternoon. They sat and talked over endless cups of tea.

'We nearly burned the kettle out,' smiled Michael.

Two days later, Michael had another day off work and came to visit again. This time he stayed until Margaret's children returned from school. Again, it seemed, the chemistry was right.

'I felt I was able to talk to them in much the same way I talk to my own daughter,' Michael recollected. 'They were very friendly to me, and I got the impression they liked me.'

Very soon, Michael and Margaret were seeing each other almost every evening. They decided it was time Margaret met Julie. 'They got on like the proverbial house on fire,' Michael recalled happily.

He had been a little apprehensive about the meeting, but his fears were swiftly dispelled. On only their second meeting, Margaret and Julie decided to go out shopping together – and left Michael at home.

Within two weeks, Margaret and Michael were discussing marriage.

'It might sound a little far-fetched – people say they don't believe in love at first sight – but it took me only about a week to fall in love with Margaret.'

'It took me only a week to fall in love.'

They both agreed that they would like to settle down with each other – and not only because the principle of doing so was attractive. They were both, quite simply, very much in love. It was Michael's suggestion that, even though they had known each other only a fortnight, they should get engaged and carry on from there.

They were formally engaged on Margaret's birthday – with plans for marriage very soon.

In the mean time, Margaret and her family have moved in with Michael and Julie. The couple gave the move a great deal of thought beforehand and, as Margaret put it: 'I felt this was what I had waited for. It just seemed right.'

David and Judith

Four lonely years passed for Judith Price following the break-up of her marriage before she finally summoned up the will to join Dateline. A thirty-one-year-old nurse living in Leeds with her daughter Lindsay, aged six,

Judith's personal confidence had been at a low ebb ever since the heartbreak of her divorce.

But she knew she must do something about making a fresh start, and with the help and much-needed encouragement of a friend, she joined.

'I was terrified when the Dateline list came through,' she said with a smile, 'because I knew I would have to do something about it!'

One particular name on that list seemed to stand out from the rest. To this day, Judith cannot say why he was the one – the only one – she chose to telephone.

'I just kept coming back to his name,' she said.

'Please don't ask who's calling. I daren't tell you.'

That name was David Newton.

David, also thirty-one, worked as a storekeeper at Burnley Hospital – where Judith had once been a nurse, though the two had never met there. He found, indeed, that his particular job was a positive social disadvantage, as it did not bring him into any contact whatever with the countless eligible young women on the nursing staff.

'I had got into a bit of a social rut,' David explained. 'Most of my friends were married, too.'

He had been out with a number of women by the time Judith's call came through.

Unhappily for Judith, who was highly nervous about making the call, David was not available.

'His mother answered and said he was out. I remember thinking, "Please don't ask who's calling, because I daren't tell you!"'

Judith said she would ring back on the following Sunday night.

'This time his mother answered again – and said he was in. That made me feel even worse! I could hear his footsteps coming to the phone.'

Judith's nerves, a bad line and the fact that she and David lived fifty miles apart could well have conspired to end the relationship there and then. But by a fortunate coincidence, Judith had already arranged to visit Burnley to stay with friends for five days – and the couple agreed that this would provide a very convenient opportunity for them to meet. (Judith, incidentally, blames her appalling geography for the fact that she requested Dateline contacts from the Manchester–Burnley area, not realizing this was so far from her home in Leeds. But it was a mistake which she now confesses herself very happy to have made.)

'He's very good-looking. He won't like *me*.'

The couple agreed that Judith and her friends would pick up David on the evening of her first day in Burnley, and they would make a foursome for dinner.

In the mean time, David sent Judith a photograph of himself.

'I remember thinking, "Crikey, he's all right. He's very good-looking. He won't like *me*!"' laughed Judith. 'On the telephone to him I'd been telling him, "I'm larger than life, you know. I'm not a slim little thing." But he had just laughed at that and said it was OK.'

All the same, Judith was apprehensive about their first meeting.

'I thought Judith was very nice, but at first things were a little tense,' David remembered of the occasion. 'She mainly talked to her friend about nursing days. But when we were having the meal things got more relaxed.'

'We got on so well, we never stopped talking,' Judith recalled. 'I thought he was lovely!'

During the following days, the couple spent every available minute together. Judith's only regret was that David had to go to work. On the last day, he took the morning off to travel home with her. As soon as her front door closed behind him when he finally left, she found herself missing him.

'When he goes home I feel as if half of me is gone.'

'When he left I knew I didn't feel complete. When he's here at the weekends I'm fine, but when he goes back home I feel as if half of me is gone. That's how I have felt from the beginning.'

The relationship deepened rapidly.

'We had so much in common,' said David. 'We think alike. We just couldn't see enough of each other.'

David spent a lot of time getting to know Lindsay.

'Considering that he hasn't had children of his own, and hasn't really mixed with any children, he gets on with her so well,' said Judith. 'I think it was strange at first for Lindsay because she's had me to herself for four years. But David makes such a fuss of her. She's looking forward to the wedding.'

It was three months after that first, awkward encounter that the couple became engaged. They plan to marry within the next year.

Judith is very happy indeed that she made that first, nerve-racking call.

'I just daren't think of what would have happened if I hadn't rung David. I think you've got to make that effort. You've joined Dateline. You've paid that money to do something about your situation. It's silly to think that you're sitting at home and all you have to do is make a phone call. It's the best phone call I ever made!'

Ron and Shirley

Nine years after her divorce, Shirley Lascelles knew the time had come to find someone to share her life with. She was tired of being on her own. Despairing of 'singles' clubs ('the only men I ever met were married'), Shirley joined Dateline.

'I had about six phone calls from chaps,' said Shirley, fifty. 'A lot of them were bachelors, and I think some had decided they wanted to get married because mum had gone and they wanted someone to care for them!'

Shirley preferred to meet people away from her home in Hampton, Surrey. This did, however, make life a little difficult, as she was uneasy about meeting men in pubs. On one occasion, she even took her son with her to the pub at which she had agreed to rendezvous.

'But with Ron,' she said with a smile, 'it was different. He insisted on picking me up.'

Fifty-eight-year-old Ron Woods from Wallington in Surrey had joined Dateline because, as he candidly admitted, he was lonely. After thirty-six years of happy marriage his wife had died, leaving him with three grown-up sons and one daughter – plus six grandchildren. But even this lively family couldn't fully console him for the gap in his life left by his wife's death.

Ron was determined not to resign himself to loneliness, and had met several women through Dateline before he contacted Shirley.

'With Ron, it was different.'

They arranged that he should pick her up at her house at 8.30. Ron arrived ten minutes early, and decided to wait in his car until the appointed hour before ringing the doorbell. But Shirley had seen the car pull up outside, and was puzzled that he didn't get out.

'Go and ask him if he's Ron Woods,' Shirley told her son Andrew, twenty-one, who still lived at home.

'Don't be silly,' he returned. 'You go out there.'

In the end, she did – only to meet Ron halfway to the house.

'Are you Ron Woods?'

'Yes. Are you Shirley?'

They both remember feeling rather foolish and self-conscious at their awkwardness.

Shirley was nevertheless impressed with Ron.

'He was wearing a nice suit, and I thought, "What an attractive man."'

She liked his manner, too.

'I'm a little bit worried getting in a car with a strange man,' she told him truthfully as she sat in the passenger seat.

'Don't worry about it, my dear,' replied Ron, straight-faced. 'I'll let you have my address and phone number.'

The evening was a success from that moment on.

'It was as if we had known each other for years,' said Ron.

'It was as if we had known each other for years.'

More dates followed, and at Christmas a few weeks later, Ron spent a good deal of time with Shirley and her family. He got to know her son Andrew better; Ron's easy manner and keen sense of humour meant that he and the young man – who was naturally protective towards his mother – were soon the best of friends.

For Ron, it was a marvellous Christmas. He enjoyed Shirley's company so much that he made up his mind she was the woman for him. He was determined to win her over.

In the new year, Ron told Shirley he would like her to have a ring that had been his wife's. She was very happy to accept it, but told him she would like the stones to be in a different setting so that she could feel it was truly hers.

Ron realized that, even now, Shirley did not feel completely committed to him. But he went ahead and had the ring remade. It was a Saturday in April when he rang her to say that he had collected the ring.

'Look, we've got to make a commitment,' he insisted. 'Either you want to marry me or you don't.'

Shirley wavered. She wanted time to think. It was more than a week later that she made up her mind.

Yes, she told Ron. She would very much like to marry him.

'Right,' said her delighted suitor. 'I'll propose properly.'

'We have a lot of laughter.'

He put on his best suit, and appeared at Shirley's house armed with a large bunch of roses, and the ring. She was in the kitchen when he arrived, so the kitchen it had to be. He handed her the roses, went promptly down on one knee and said with due gravity: 'Shirley, will you marry me?'

'She nearly crushed me when she fell on me,' laughed Ron.

They were married at a spiritualist church in Hampton Hill, just a little less than a year after their first meeting. Between them they now have six children, all of whom think their marriage has been a wonderful thing for both of them – and happy confirmation that computer dating does not work exclusively for the young.

'We have a lot of laughter,' said Ron. 'This is one of the beauties of our marriage. I've been getting told off by Andrew for getting up in the morning at 7.30 and singing my head off. He's a right misery in the morning!'

Shirley, for all her natural caution, was not really

surprised at the speed of her attachment to Ron. She cannot remember exactly when it was she realized she had fallen in love, but she had very quickly discovered she couldn't imagine life without him.

'He takes care of me,' she says simply. 'He is *so* good.'

Colin and Pauline

Pauline Anderson and Colin Santer had common reasons for joining Dateline. Both were newly divorced, but unhappy being on their own. Neither found it easy to get out and meet new people.

'I was a bit frightened about what sort of people I'd meet.'

Thirty-year-old Pauline was cautious about joining: 'I was just a bit dubious. A bit frightened about what sort of people I'd meet.'

Egged on by her friends at the hospital where she worked as an auxiliary nurse, Pauline finally plucked up the courage. She met three contacts before Colin.

'One I was seeing for five months,' she said. 'But he just wanted a good friendship. We used to play squash and badminton together and go out in a crowd. I wanted something more permanent.'

So the friendship ended, by mutual consent. Working nights, and a lack of new contacts through Dateline, meant this was a low patch for Pauline. Then, one morning when she returned from work, there was a letter on the mat. It was from Colin Santer.

'It really cheered me up,' remembers Pauline. 'It was quite funny.'

That night at work, she wrote back.

Colin, also thirty and an electronics engineer, was delighted with Pauline's prompt reply. He had only just joined Dateline and she was on his first list of names. She was destined to be the only one of those names he would meet.

By telephone, Colin arranged to see Pauline in Worthing, Sussex, where she lived, the following weekend – which happened to be Easter.

'Colin made me feel at ease.'

The weather turned out to be typically unkind, especially for Colin, who decided to motorcycle from his home in Tunbridge Wells, Kent.

'It was one of the worst days for motorcycling I can ever remember,' said Colin. 'It rained and snowed and blew all the way down. I got absolutely drowned.'

Bedraggled as he was by the time he reached his destination, Colin nevertheless spent a fruitful day with Pauline and her twelve-year-old daughter, Michelle. He had thoughtfully brought an Easter egg, and also photographs of his children. Michelle – to her mother's embarrassment – brought out all their family photos too.

'I very much enjoyed that day,' said Pauline. 'Colin made me feel very much at ease.'

By the end of the day, they had agreed that they should meet again, and made arrangements for the following weekend. But when Colin rang in midweek to confirm, he had an unpleasant surprise – a message that Pauline had gone to her mother's.

'I thought perhaps she didn't want to see me any more and didn't want to have to say so to my face,' Colin recalled.

Happily, his fears were unfounded. Pauline rang the next day to explain that her sudden departure had been a mission of mercy to her mother, who had been taken ill.

Relieved as he was, Colin's next meeting with Pauline had another surprise in store for him – on the squash court.

'I beat him easily. Hands down!' Pauline remembered with a laugh. 'He had said he could play, but he couldn't really.'

'We were made for each other.'

They began to meet more often, and soon realized how much they meant to one another.

'She has this terrific sense of humour,' said Colin. 'We seemed to have so much in common.'

'We got on really well together,' Pauline agreed. 'He didn't take me for granted. He just made me feel wanted. He treated me as a woman.'

They decided to spend a 'trial weekend' together in Tunbridge Wells, while Michelle was staying with her father. Colin took Pauline to have supper with his mother, and as soon as they got home to his flat – before even switching a light on – he asked Pauline to marry him.

'If you're going to ask me you'd better get down on one knee,' Pauline told him.

In the pitch dark of the flat, Colin promptly did so, and made his proposal with due ceremony – in spite of the fact that his intended bride could not even see him.

They had first met only six weeks before, but Pauline had no hesitation in accepting.

'It was just as if we were made for each other.'

Pauline and Colin were married at Tunbridge Wells Register Office three months later and they now live in Pauline's Worthing home.

Jon and Lesley

Twin girls of eleven and a seven-year-old son kept Lesley Raper hard at work at home in Bude, Cornwall – and made it less than easy for the thirty-two-year-old divorcee to get out and meet people. So, after much heart-searching, she decided to join Dateline.

'I get awfully tongue-tied.'

One week after she did so, Jon Glencross, also thirty-two, a farmer from Liskeard, thirty-eight miles away, did the same.

'I'd heard about Dateline on Radio Luxembourg,' he said. 'I was fed up not meeting anyone locally, and I don't enjoy going into pubs on my own.'

Lesley's name appeared on the first list of introductions he was sent. He wrote to her, as well as to the others.

'It was a very interesting letter,' Lesley recalled. 'And quite amusing. We did seem to have a lot in common – our interests, and both coming from the country. So I wrote back.'

So began a correspondence which lasted for a number of weeks, in the process of which they got to know each other quite well. They didn't use the telephone at all.

'With complete strangers, I'm all right on the phone,' Jon admitted. 'But with anyone I'm starting to get to know, I get awfully tongue-tied.'

It was Jon who suggested in one letter that the time had come for them to meet. In her reply, Lesley invited him to come and see her at home.

'He came on a Saturday when I was at home with the children,' she recalled. 'I was extremely nervous, but when I met him I thought at once how nice he was. He seemed outgoing, and he did put me at my ease.'

'I knew that if she didn't do the talking I would clam right up too!'

'I was terrified,' Jon admitted with a grin. 'A bag of nerves. On the way there I was wondering whether I'd done the right thing. I wondered, too, whether she was one of those people who just join Dateline for a laugh. I knew that if she didn't do the talking I would clam right up too!'

But he need not have worried. Lesley's children gave them no opportunity to sit in embarrassed silence.

'They were a bit uncontrollable that day,' laughed Lesley. 'They weren't used to seeing a man in the house, and they were all over the place!'

She and Jon managed to escape to a nearby pub for a break from the din. Having a son of his own from his previous marriage, Jon was not overwhelmed by Lesley's children, and they found they had plenty to talk about.

Jon nevertheless sensed a slight reserve in Lesley as they sat in the pub. He concluded that she couldn't think much of him. 'She won't want to see me again,' he thought to himself.

When he took her home he was surprised, therefore, when she invited him in for coffee.

Now, on her home territory and with the children in bed, Lesley relaxed much more. For the next four hours, they really talked, and Jon was able confidently to ask her if she would see him again.

'She accepted my way of life – which helped tremendously.'

The sun was up by the time Jon got home, and he did his early morning work on the land – his head full of happy thoughts – before finally falling into bed.

He returned to Lesley's two days later, and to the relief of both of them her children were much less excitable. It was soon apparent to the couple that they were at the beginning of something long-term.

'Everything seemed to be going right,' Lesley remembered.

'Always before when I had been with somebody I'd have a nagging doubt inside,' said Jon. 'But this time I've not had that feeling. Lesley liked the country, and accepted my way of life – which helped tremendously.'

*

It was a summer's evening, some four months after their first exchange of letters, that Lesley and Jon found themselves in a not-altogether-romantic setting – on a seat in a town car park, thoroughly enjoying a bag of sausages and chips. But they had spent a memorable happy evening together, and John had realized with sudden clarity just how much he wanted their happiness to continue.

Without warning, he slid off the seat and on to one knee.

'Will you have me?' he solemnly asked the astonished Lesley.

'I hadn't expected her to say yes,' he admitted, 'But she did!'

Dee and Roger

On the surface, Roger and Dee are two very different people. He is quiet, outwardly calm. She is a chatty and extrovert woman. But it is obvious, seeing them together in their roomy home at Ewell in Surrey, just how admirably well suited to each other they are.

Before she met Roger through Dateline, Dee had spent four years alone, following her divorce.

'I was working nights at British Telecom,' said Dee, an attractive woman just into her forties, 'and teaching music part-time.'

This meant her social life was difficult to plan.

'I *was* going out – but I was fed up with meeting other women's husbands; men who were really only after a one-night stand,' she said in her characteristically forthright manner.

A friend talked Dee into joining Dateline. She mulled over the questionnaire for a long time before filling it in (she cheerfully admitted to chopping a few years off her age) and taking the plunge.

Dee had seven or eight dates before she met Roger.

'On the whole they were all nice, and I did have things in common with them. But the chemistry wasn't there. It was great fun, though. Never a dull moment.'

She was actually giving Dateline a bit of a rest when Roger rang – having been given her name on his list.

'I was fed up with meeting other women's husbands.'

'I didn't really want to speak to him,' said Dee. 'But my eldest daughter, who was living with me at the time, answered the phone and said he sounded nice. She more or less forced me to talk to him.'

Despite her dismissive tone, Roger succeeded in making a date with Dee.

'I did wonder what she must be like,' he admitted. 'She had been up all night at work, smoking far too much, and all I could hear was this terribly croaky voice!'

Roger, a thirty-eight-year-old businessman with his own flourishing contract flooring company, took up the story.

'I had been divorced for some time, but hadn't had much chance to get lonely, because I was building up my business. On my last birthday, however, I was having a solitary drink and it just struck me that I ought to join Dateline.'

Without further ado, he wrote off for details, and joined.

'It was done with the attitude, "Nothing ventured, nothing gained",' he said. 'I certainly wasn't going to spend months sitting in my flat working and doing little else.'

When he received his first list of six names, Roger hesitated. He waited a week before doing anything about it.

'In the end, one evening I told myself, "It's got to be done. The people on that piece of paper are in the same situation as you. They have joined because they want to meet someone."'

'All I could hear was this terribly croaky voice.'

So he sat down with a bottle of wine, and dialled the first number.

'By the time I got to number five, I was getting quite blasé about the whole thing – because I had such a good reception.'

Roger had a number of dates, some of whom he saw several times before he first met Dee.

'We swapped car numbers so we could recognize each other when we met,' said Dee. 'I liked his looks immediately – I love beards!'

Roger admitted that he was a little amazed by his first encounter with Dee.

'I was unprepared for the overall effect,' he said with a laugh. 'The blonde hair, the sun tan. I was bowled over!'

Dee was in no doubt that she wanted to see Roger again. She suggested the next *three* evenings.

Roger wasn't so sure.

'I found her rather overpowering,' he said, 'so I made excuses.'

But that weekend, alone in his flat, Roger found himself regretting those excuses, and thinking, 'Why am I sitting here on my own when I could have been meeting Dee?'

'I found her rather overpowering.'

So he bought some tickets for a Jasper Carrott show and telephoned Dee at work.

'We had a wonderful evening,' she said. 'And with very few exceptions we've been together ever since.'

The couple never became formally engaged. Five months after their first meeting, Roger simply told her, 'We're going out to get you a ring,' and they were married three months after that in the local Register Office.

'I'm now very much more relaxed,' said Dee. 'Roger and I are together nearly all the time. I no longer work for British Telecom, but help Roger with the business instead.

'I took sleeping pills for twenty years,' she continued, 'and now I don't have to take them any more. Now there's always something to look forward to and there are never enough hours in the day. I'm always behind with everything on the house, but it doesn't seem to matter. Roger helps even though he's so busy with his work. He's marvellously organized, even if I'm not!'

Roger and Dee are a very happy example of the fact that you do not have to be alike to be compatible. Both of them agree, however, that without the help of the computer, their utterly different lifestyles would have prevented them from ever meeting. And that would have been sad indeed.

7

Starting over – after bereavement

For those who lose a partner through death, the world changes. The secure supports that sustain life through a loving relationship are swept away. The surviving partner feels defenceless, abandoned.

In the early days of being widowed, the all-consuming need to grieve leaves little energy – physical or spiritual – with which to foster new friendships. The labour of mourning is exacting.

But gradually the pain of loss does lessen. A sense of new purpose does emerge. The task of merely surviving turns to one of living again.

For some who are widowed, the memory of the lost partner makes any thought of another intimate relationship distasteful. For others, the re-emerging need for love and sexual closeness comes as a surprise – and poses a dilemma.

After years of comfortable togetherness within a known and secure relationship, the ability to acquire and sustain new friends is neither as easy nor as spontaneous as once it was. In the second-time-around age group, there may be fewer social settings which offer an opportunity to meet a potential mate. And the lack of confidence can make facing a gathering of strangers a terrible ordeal.

This is particularly true for widows – of whom only a very small proportion ever remarry.

When the normal channels through which lovers meet and marry are limited, the longing for close companionship may encourage bereaved people to use the services of marriage bureaux or introduction agencies. Responsible bureaux will not accept on to their books a new widow or widower until they are confident that the party concerned is seeking a new partner – and not simply a replica of the one that has been lost. Unless a person is chosen for his or her individual qualities, the chances of a new marriage succeeding are less than good.

The expectations both partners bring to a new relationship may need to be clarified. These do not always coincide – and the yearning for companionship may, for a while, obscure very real differences.

Less obvious – but no less real – may be the more deeply hidden feelings of disloyalty to the dead partner which can subtly sabotage a new relationship. These need to be brought out into the open, for any second marriage in the circumstances must candidly accommodate the emotional 'luggage' of the past.

A good, well-founded match will be enhanced and strengthened by past experience. An ill-based one will be undermined by the failure to acknowledge that past experience contributes much to the way we are.

For those who do find happiness and contentment in second marriages, the rewards far outweigh the risks. A widow expressed the feelings of countless others in a letter she wrote to Cruse, the National Organization for the Widowed and their Children.

This has been a wonderfully happy year for my new husband and me.

We had both known great happiness in our former marriages and neither of us had thought of remarrying. It is wonderful to know the joy of caring and sharing again. After several years on our own we have had no difficulties in adjusting to a new life together.

Looking back, I have been trying to think what basic qualities were necessary to 'make' our second marriage.

I think kindness and sensitivity are most important because, in trying to make our two homes fit into one, a great deal of sorting out had to be done. It would have been terribly easy to hurt one another by insisting that some item wouldn't fit in. We just took our time in working through things, and each kept many things we felt we just couldn't part with.

Then there was the dog – which could have been a difficulty. But we have incorporated her into the household and I have become very fond of her.

I have come to realize that if you really love one another then your great aim is to make the other happy. In doing this, you experience great happiness yourself.

— WENDY WILSON, CRUSE

Cruse was founded in 1959, and is a registered charity with more than 100 branches in Britain. Headquarters: Cruse House, 126 Sheen Road, Richmond, Surrey TW9 1UR. Telephone: 01-940 4818/9047.

Audrey and Chris

A year and a day after Christopher Bird's wife died, he received a note from his bank manager. With it came a letter, written by his wife before her death and handed to the bank for safekeeping until that day.

'It was a lovely letter, and a poem, "The Unquiet Grave", said Chris. 'She thanked me for so many wonderful years . . . and said that I should carry on with my life.'

Profoundly affected by the letter, Chris, aged sixty, knew he must indeed carry on; he knew only too well that to his year-long sadness was being added the extra pain of loneliness. Encouraged by his grown-up children, Chris decided to join Dateline.

His first list of names came through. Of the six, he chose to write first to Audrey Hutt. She lived in Crowborough, East Sussex, and thus was furthest away of any of the six from Chris's home in Romford, Essex.

'I don't know to this day why I picked out Audrey,' he said. 'For some unknown reason I thought, "That's the lady I'm going to contact first."'

Audrey had been widowed eighteen months. It had been a difficult time.

'I've got four children – three of them married – and we are a close family. They tried to include me in things,' she said. 'But it's never the same as your own partner. After a happy marriage of thirty-six years there is that void there. Of companionship, someone to talk to and plan things with. And I knew that I was just basically not a loner.'

It was Audrey's daughter who egged her into sending for details of Dateline.

Audrey was doubtful: 'I don't know whether I've got the courage to meet people in that way,' she confessed to her daughter.

'Well, there are so many people in this particular position,' came the reply. 'The people who join are not messing around, they're all serious about it.'

Persuaded, Audrey sent off for a Dateline Free Computer Test and, when the results came, she decided to join. In what was turning out to be a real family effort, her eldest son now helped her fill out the comprehensive questionnaire – and Audrey took the plunge.

'In the beginning I thought it would be nice to meet

**'The people who join are not messing around.
They're all serious about it.'**

---

someone to go to the theatre with,' she remembered. 'I didn't think I would get married again. In my day, you had an engagement which lasted for two or three years and then you got married.'

Audrey liked the letter she received from Chris.

'It was very nice, and to the point. I felt that this was someone I could trust myself to meet.'

By this stage, Audrey had met four men through Dateline. ('All of them very nice, but there was no spark there.')

On the evening of Easter Monday, she sat down to write back to Chris. When she had written the letter, she remained sitting a while, looking at it. On Chris's letter, she saw he had put his telephone number. On the spur of the moment, she decided to call him instead.

Chris was delighted to hear from her.

'On that Monday I was feeling very lonely,' he recalled. 'It was 9.30 in the evening and I was so pleased to get a call.'

They got on very well, and arranged to meet for dinner the following week.

'I liked the sound of his voice. He sounded very genuine and sincere.'

'She sounded so sincere and happy. She didn't sound nervous, although she said she was. I knew I wanted to meet her.'

'I felt that this was someone I could trust myself to meet.'

They met at the station in Sevenoaks, Kent. She had described what she would be wearing. He would be easy to spot, as he was six-foot-two.

But Chris nearly walked straight past her. There was no one else about, but surely this lady looked too young to be Audrey Hutt? Yet it had to be her.

'Audrey?' he asked her.

'Yes. Chris?'

Audrey found herself facing this tall, slim, smiling man.

They passed a happy evening in a local steak house, enjoying talking about themselves, about each other, about their families.

But when they parted, Chris didn't attempt to make an arrangement to meet again.

'I felt at that time that maybe he wasn't ready to be committed any further than one evening – and I didn't want to push him,' said Audrey. 'When I said goodbye, I said "Good hunting" or something like that.'

Audrey's instincts were correct – partly. Chris had wanted to go home and think things over.

'The very next day I made up my mind that she was a woman I wanted to see more of,' he said. 'Then just as I was going to sit down and write another letter to her, she telephoned me.'

Audrey, too, was going to write, to thank Chris for their enjoyable evening. But she decided to phone again instead.

'I didn't expect her to say yes.'

And Chris again was thrilled to hear from her. They arranged another dinner at the same venue.

It was on their third meeting that Chris suddenly realized how fond he was becoming of Audrey. Then, in May, she had to go to Holland for a while, and he discovered just how much he missed her. He had, until then, believed that he was not yet ready for a strong relationship. Now he felt differently.

On her return, Audrey invited him to her home.

'I was so happy on that occasion,' Chris recalled. 'I knew Audrey was the lady I wanted to spend the rest of my life with.'

They went out for dinner, but came back to her house for coffee. Chris knew he must speak his mind.

'I've got something to ask you,' he told Audrey. 'Would you marry me?'

'Quite frankly,' he recollected, 'I didn't expect her to say yes. I thought she might feel I was rushing things a little bit. But to my delight she *did* say yes.'

Although it was indeed only a short time since they had met, neither of them was in any doubt that marriage was what they wanted.

But such a whirlwind courtship meant that Audrey and Chris had done little to keep their families informed. Audrey's children were dumfounded.

'My daughter was rather quiet about it when I told her on the phone,' said Audrey. 'She said, "My mother's going to marry someone I've never even met!"'.

It took only their first meeting for Audrey's daughter and Chris to solve that area of concern, for the two of them got on fine.

'My mother's going to marry someone I've never even met.'

'I know he'll look after you, Mum,' she said. 'He's very sweet and I'm sure you'll be very happy.'

Chris's family, having had a hint or two from their father in advance that he thought he had met the woman he hoped to spend the rest of his life with, were delighted.

'If you feel like that,' his daughter had told him, 'go ahead. Grab her!'

Audrey and Chris were married in July, just about four months after they first met. Their Register Office wedding was followed by a church blessing – and an unforgettable honeymoon in Corsica.

'We just keep telling each other how lucky we are, because we both had happy first marriages,' said Audrey. 'To think we could be blessed twice is almost incredible, because we are very, very happy. We feel very, very well blessed.'

Ivor and Pamela

For three years Pamela Breen was both mother and father to her teenage daughters. She and Jeanette, eighteen, Marianne, sixteen, and Linda, fourteen, lived a close-knit life together in their Leeds home. It was an all-female family, even down to the dog, Penny.

But Pamela knew in her heart that something was missing.

'I had been a widow for three years,' she explained. 'My children were coming up to leaving school and I didn't want to be one of those mothers who clung to them.'

Pamela knew that at forty she was still young enough to make a new life for herself. She felt it was high time she met another man and settled down with him. She was very conscious, too, that the longer she left it, the harder it would be.

'I felt that I was wasted on my own.'

'I felt that I was wasted on my own because I liked having someone around to look after. Not that I'm really a social person – I'd rather visit friends at home than go out.'

Having three daughters, said Pamela, she was anxious not 'to get mixed up with the wrong sort of person. I thought about Dateline and decided it would be the best way of meeting someone respectable.'

One of the names Pamela received on joining was that of Ivor Clark, a forty-five-year-old nurse from Huddersfield. He had been a Dateline member just a week short of a year. Had Pamela delayed joining by just that one week, she and Ivor would never have met.

Her letter reached Ivor shortly before he was due to go on holiday. He wrote directly back to tell her this. It did occur to Pamela that he might be making up an excuse not to meet her, but she wrote back none the less, suggesting they should meet when Ivor returned from holiday.

Now, at the last minute, Ivor rang her up to say there was just time for them to meet before he went away. Meet they did – at Leeds Station.

'I decided Dateline would be the best way of meeting someone respectable.'

'I had an idea of what she looked like from her description in her letter,' said Ivor. 'When I saw her I thought what a nice-looking lady she was.'

Despite being very shy, Ivor went up to her at once.

'This stranger approached me a bit hesitantly,' Pamela recalled. 'He asked me if I was Pam.'

To Ivor's intense relief, she affirmed that she was.

By the evening's end, the couple were in no doubt that they wished to see each other again. Ivor promised to phone the minute he returned.

This he did, and the couple readily took up their budding relationship again.

If Pamela had any doubts, one was that Ivor was a very quiet man. This suited her, but how on earth, she wondered, would he get on with her three lively daughters?

When they did all meet, Pamela discovered she need never have worried. The girls accepted him as quickly as he accepted them.

'We all seem to get on OK,' said Ivor with typical understatement. 'We got on very nicely.'

Pamela was delighted with the way he just seemed to merge in with the family.

'Even the dog loves him!' she laughed.

Ivor proposed to Pamela three months after their first meeting. But she didn't accept him immediately.

'Even the dog loves him!'

'I felt we ought to hang on, because he was taking on a lot more than I was,' she explained.

But Ivor quietly persevered, and after four months more, the couple were married at Leeds Register Office.

David and Heather

Widowed at the age of just twenty-seven, Heather Whyte resolved after a year that she must get out and meet men again. She began by answering two advertisements in her local paper, the Edinburgh *Evening News*.

'They were both an absolute disaster,' she recalled ruefully.

She joined Dateline at the suggestion of a friend – but after some hesitation.

'I joined to meet different people at the start,' she said.

'But gradually I got to the stage where I wanted to meet somebody who I could start all over again with. I've actually been married twice. My first marriage ended in divorce and my second husband died. I wanted to find somebody to bring me out of myself.'

Heather had been out with five different people before she was telephoned by Davie Roe, a twenty-nine-year-old joiner who also lived in Edinburgh.

'I was on edge waiting to hear from him.'

'He spoke to my mum first, and she told me he would be phoning back as I was out. I was on edge waiting to hear from him. I looked him up in the Edinburgh telephone directory to see what sort of area he lived in – but he's not in the phone book!'

When David phoned back, she was not unpleasantly surprised.

'He was very easy to talk to – we spent an hour chatting.'

For David, Heather was his first Dateline contact. It was his job – he worked for himself – that was behind his joining.

'I was working long hours,' he explained. 'So I was finding it pretty difficult to meet the right sort of woman.'

David admitted that it was 'a wee while' before he joined. 'I was fed up being by myself with no company, but I nevertheless had second thoughts about joining.'

The lack of girlfriends did, fortunately for him, outweigh his apprehension. Heather was destined to be the only one of his Dateline contacts he would meet, and he was as delighted with their first telephone talk as she was.

When they did meet, Heather admitted to being a little surprised by him.

'When you talk to somebody on the phone, you try to picture what he's going to be like – but David wasn't the least like I had expected. But during the course of

---

'David wasn't the least like I'd expected.'

---

the evening I found him very easy to talk to and very charming. He's a thorough gentleman.'

They both readily agreed to another date.

'I was very taken with her from the first,' said David. 'We just seemed to have everything in common.'

'I really never thought it would work.'

It was a few months after their first date that the couple spent a week together in the north of Scotland – and discovered how naturally compatible they were.

'I don't like cooking, for instance,' said Heather. 'So he did it – and I did the driving.'

They were at David's flat, just after the holiday, when he proposed. They agreed to become formally engaged at Hogmanay.

As soon as midnight struck, Dave put a ring on Heather's finger, and she slipped one on his.

*

They plan to marry in the near future, and in the mean time both express delight at having discovered one another.

'Compared to a year ago. my life is just brilliant now,' says Heather.

David cheerfully admits his astonishment at his good fortune in joining Dateline.

'I really never thought it would work!' he confesses.

Barbara and Bill

A year of being a widow convinced Barbara, who was in her mid-forties, that she did not wish to spend the rest of her life alone. She knew the time had come to look for companionship.

'To be honest, I was lonely.'

Her Dateline membership got off to a slow start. The first two names she was sent did not even reply to her letters. But she was determined to persevere.

'It was third time lucky,' she said, smiling at her new husband. 'It was Bill.'

Bill, a fifty-year-old, quiet-spoken Midlander, smiled back.

'I was divorced and had been on my own for seven years. To be honest, I was lonely. I had been on holiday alone and wished I had had company.'

On joining Dateline, Bill had been sent six names, but none had worked out. Then he received Barbara's letter.

114

'He phoned me up,' said Barbara, 'and asked if I would like to exchange photographs.'

They did so, and subsequently wrote to each other several times, as well as speaking on the phone. Finally, they decided to meet. Bill was to travel to Barbara's home in Essex.

'I met him at the station,' she remembered. Then, rather shyly, she admitted, 'I know first impressions don't count, but ... well ... it was love at first sight!'

Barbara laughed self-consciously.

'It's true,' said Bill. 'We got on very well on the telephone, and it was just like a magnet when we met. I'm normally a shy man – but we weren't shy with each other at all.'

'It was just like a magnet when we met.'

So successful was that first meeting that they promptly decided to spend Christmas together. In the intervening month, they spoke daily on the phone, and continued to correspond regularly.

'In the end we decided not to waste time,' Bill remembered happily. 'There didn't seem any point in a long-term courtship!'

Christmas was memorable indeed, for Barbara and Bill were married at the Southend Register Office on 29 December. Barbara moved back to the Midlands with Bill.

What of her desire merely for 'companionship'?

Barbara laughed. 'We love each other. I've got much more than companionship!'

What of the old saying, 'Marry in haste – repent at leisure'?

'Well, I'm not repenting,' said Bill. 'I'm truly content – and I would advise anyone to do as I have.'

How Dateline can work for you

Dateline is the largest and most successful computer dating company in the world and this, together with its unique computerised matching system, is the secret of its success. There really is no better way to meet so many unattached people – all of them matched on specific criteria and all of them with one common aim – a close and loving relationship.

More than 35,000 men and women join Dateline every year. For each of them it was a personal decision to do something positive about finding someone special. If you would like to do the same simply contact

Dateline
23 Abingdon Road
London W8 6AH
Tel: 01 938 1011